The
SONG of LIFE
HEALING MATRIX

Transcendence
TOOLBOOKS
Experience Beyond Words

Transcendence Toolbooks, vol 2

The
SONG of LIFE
HEALING MATRIX

_____

KIM MICHAELS

For information and foreign rights, contact:

MORE TO LIFE PUBLISHING

Website: www.morepublish.com

E-mail: info@morepublish.com

ISBN: 978-9949-518-16-6

Transcendence Toolbooks series ISBN: 978-9949-518-04-3

Cover and interior design: Helen Michaels

CONTENTS

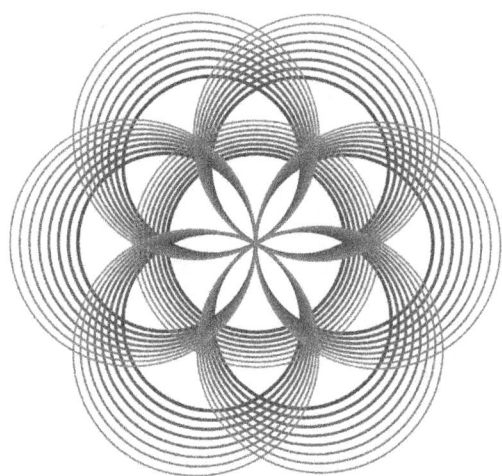

INTRODUCTION

The Song of Life Healing Matrix is designed to help you heal any condition in your life, including physical illness, emotional wounds, mental limitations and even your sense of identity. It will also help you heal the deeper issues of who you are, why you are in existence as a self-aware being and why you are here on earth.

This book contains a unique combination of teachings and practical tools for invoking spiritual light. Both the teachings and the invocations are given by the universal spiritual teachers of humankind, also known as the ascended masters. The teachings and tools in this book are given by the feminine representatives of the ascended masters, those who hold the Office of the Divine Mother for planet earth. This makes the Healing Matrix very practical for healing any imbalanced condition you deal with in the material world, even helping you develop the mastery of mind over matter.

If you are not familiar with the ascended masters and their teachings, it is recommended that you read the book *The Power of Self*, which explains who the masters are, how they can help you and how you can follow the path to self-mastery offered by the masters. You can also find information on the website: *www.ascendedmasterlight.com*.

The invocations and decrees in Part Two are meant to be read aloud by you. You can read them in a slow, meditative way or you can give them faster and with more power in your voice. There is no one right way to give the invocations, but they obviously cannot work with full power unless you read them aloud. If you desire more detailed instructions for how to give invocations, please visit the website: *www.transcendencetoolbox.com*. You might also find it helpful to give the invocations along with a recording. You can purchase and download sound files of the invocations from the website: *www.morepublish.com*. You can also purchase sound files of the teaching chapters. You will find that listening to a sound file carries a greater amount of spiritual light, released through the spoken word.

It is suggested that you start using this book by reading the first chapter and then giving the first invocation (found in Part Two). You can then move on to the second chapter and so on until you have given all eight invocations. Once you are familiar with the teachings, you do not have to read the chapter before giving an invocation, yet you will probably find that doing so helps you get more out of giving the invocation.

There is no right or wrong way to use the invocations and the decrees. As one example, you might give one invocation per day until you have given all eight and then start over. You might do this four times, which takes a little over a month, and this will give you a good feel for the power of this ritual. You can, of course, continue this daily ritual for as long as you like.

It is recommended that you use your intuition to sense how you can best adapt the tools to your personal situation. You might be prompted from within to give one particular invocation every day until you feel you have gained the result you need at this time.

Depending on your speed, it takes 15-25 minutes to give one invocation. This means you can give all eight invocations (one after the other) in a little over two hours, which is a very powerful ritual. If you decide to do this, you do not have to give the opening prayer or the sealing with each invocation. You give an opening prayer when you start and the sealing after you finish the last invocation.

After each invocation you will find the decree that is used in that invocation. You can use this decree as a stand-alone tool for invoking light from the particular lady master who released the decree. A decree can be given faster and with a more powerful rhythm than an invocation, and you can give it a number of times, such as 9 times or 36 times. You can also give the decree a number of times at the end of an invocation, before giving the sealing. Don't be afraid to be creative in the use of the tools included in the healing matrix. For example, you can give the matrix for another person who is ill, for all persons who suffer from a particular disease or even for the healing of the collective consciousness. You can even play the recording for people who are ill.

If you make the effort to overcome your initial resistance and build a momentum on giving the Healing Matrix, you will likely find that it is one of the most powerful and effective spiritual tools you have ever used. By combining this tool with a willingness to look into your own psyche and letting go of limiting beliefs, you can turn your life into an upward spiral that will lead to the healing of any condition. Truly, as the masters say, everything revolves around your free will. If you can accept that healing is possible for you, then healing will be manifest for you. Invoke, and ye shall receive.

Part One

Teachings from the Divine Mother

Chapter 1

RECREATING YOUR SENSE OF SELF

Ma-ray-taii.
Ma-ray-taii.
Ma-ray-taii.

Maraytaii is my name. I am a representative of the Divine Mother. Whereas Mother Mary is the representative of the Divine Mother for earth, I am a representative of the Divine Mother at the galactic level for your galaxy. I am not the highest representative of the Divine Mother at the galactic level, but I am one of the representatives.

Thus, I am come to earth to bring a gift, a gift that I bring in oneness with other representatives of the Divine Mother for earth: Portia, the Goddess of Justice, Nada, the Chohan of the Sixth Ray, Kuan Yin, a representative of Divine Mercy, and of course, Mother Mary. We bring you this gift of what we have called the Song of Life.

It is a gift from the Divine Feminine to all people on earth. It has a simple purpose, and that is to give you the teachings and the practical tools to bring yourself into harmony, into synchrony, into resonance with the Song of Life. What is the Song of Life? Let me explain.

THE CREATIVE ROLE OF SOUND

The Maha Chohan in his book *[Flowing with the River of Life]* has explained how the force of the Holy Spirit has been created by self-aware beings – starting in the very first sphere – who have used their co-creative abilities to transcend their sense of self and create that which is more. The Song of Life is part of the River of Life, the movement of the Holy Spirit. But it is a specific aspect of it. For what is it that stirs the undifferentiated Ma-ter light into taking on a specific form and maintaining that form over time?

Well, it is what you on earth would call sound. And you have been given the teaching that when God started the creative process, he supposedly said: "Let there be light." But you see, this is an explanation given to human beings at a certain level of consciousness, for on earth you know that you cannot speak, you cannot create sound, unless there is a medium through which the sound can propagate.

So you see, what is stated in Genesis is not the very first act of creation. The first act of creation was to create the Ma-ter light, which is undifferentiated and has no form. This could not have been done through sound, for there was no medium through which the sound could propagate. And thus, it was done through the awareness of the Creator.

But once the Ma-ter light was brought into existence, there needs to be a force that can stir it into form and maintain that form. We have explained that you are co-creators, that you have the ability to formulate a mental image in your mind and to then superimpose or project that image upon the Ma-ter light. But how do you project an image upon the Ma-ter light? Well, you do so through what is the equivalent of sound, but which is not necessarily audible sound. It is, instead, a rhythmic movement that has certain sequences that repeat in a pattern, a matrix.

And it is this rhythmic movement that not only stirs the Ma-ter light to take on a certain form, but that gives that form a continued existence by repeating the pattern. And it is thus this repetition of the pattern that maintains the form.

YOUR MIND IS A MUSICAL INSTRUMENT

Now, you know that in order to produce sound, you need some kind of instrument. But an instrument does not have to be physical or material, for you understand, do you not, that if everything in the material world is created from sounds stirring the Ma-ter light, there could not have been a material instrument that created material form. For what would then have created that instrument when there was no form?

Thus, you see, creation starts at a higher level where your I AM Presence creates a certain sound, a certain rhythmic matrix, which it then projects into the identity level. Your identity body then becomes an instrument for amplifying and magnifying that soundless sound from your Presence and then projecting it into your mental body. Where your mental body now becomes the instrument at that level of creation, again amplifying, perhaps changing somewhat, the sound and then projecting it into the feeling body. Where your feelings might distort it even more, before it is projected onto the material level where this projection of rhythmic matrices literally forms your physical body and the state of health or unhealth of your physical body.

So going back to Genesis and the statement that God said: "Let there be light," you understand that the God referred to in

Genesis was the level of creation of the Elohim, who took the light from the etheric, the identity level, put it into rhythmic motion, then projected it into the mental, then into the emotional, and then into the physical. And then, out of the light that had now taken on the vibrations of the material spectrum, they then created the earth by again projecting a sound matrix, if you will, upon the Ma-ter light.

This is how everything has been created. This is how any form can be maintained over time, because there is a rhythmic pattern that is continually being superimposed upon the Ma-ter light, causing the Ma-ter light to maintain a certain form.

FORM IS CONSTANTLY RECREATED

But do you understand that the form, that you see in the material, does not have a continuous or self-sufficient existence? You have been brought up to think that the earth has existed for 4.5 billion years. You have been brought up to think there are distant stars and galaxies, that there are atoms and molecules, that there are many different forms that exist that have some self-sufficient existence. They exist on their own, they have an objective existence.

This is the grand illusion that humankind is coming close to being ready to question and overcome, where you realize that nothing is set in stone; nothing is permanent. For everything that you see, every form that you see, is continually being re-created through the rhythm that stirs the Ma-ter light into maintaining the form.

It is like you see in a movie theater, where you know there are individual images on a film strip, projected so quickly that your eyes do not see them as individual images but as a continuous, smooth movement. You have all seen images of the first black-

and-white movies, where people's movements were more jerky, simply because there were fewer images displayed every second. And thus, your eyes were not completely fooled into seeing it as a smooth, continuous movement. You know that movies in the beginning were called "motion pictures;" still pictures in motion. And so you see, nothing is permanent. Nothing has an independent existence, for there must be some sound, some rhythmic pattern, that maintains the form over time by being continually projected upon the Ma-ter light.

This is not to in any way frighten you. For I can assure you that there are spiritual beings who have accepted the task of maintaining the cosmic framework you have in the material universe, including planet earth. I am not trying to say here that the entire universe could suddenly disappear.

THE HOPE FOR HEALING

The purpose for us giving you this teaching is to give you hope. For when you realize that your physical body does not have a continuous, objective, independent existence, you realize that there is great hope for healing any disease in the body. Disease, even aging, is not an inevitable process that cannot be reversed. For any condition in your body is created through the rhythmic projection of patterns upon the Ma-ter light. Your physical body is the lowest level of the four levels of your being, so any manifestation in the body is projected through the identity, the mental, the emotional and the physical levels of the mind. This does mean that – many times a second – a certain, rhythmic matrix is being projected upon the Ma-ter light that makes up your physical body. And if that matrix was changed, your body would change also.

In fact, how can it be that a healthy body becomes ill? It is because the rhythmic matrix projected upon the Ma-ter light that makes up the body has changed. Instead of the more harmonious matrix of a healthy body, you now have a disharmony that creeps into the rhythmic matrix and this manifests as disease.

Your cells are not self-existent. They are amplifiers. They are tuning forks for the matrix superimposed upon them from the three higher levels of the mind. And only when a certain disharmony creeps into one or all of these levels, can there be disease at the physical level. But this also means that if you can change the disharmony and bring it back into harmony, then you can heal any condition in the body. Even aging can be reversed. Do you see the potential here?

You may have seen science fiction movies where they have a certain instrument that sends out invisible rays that can almost instantly heal the physical body. Such technology will indeed be brought forth in the not-too-distant future, at least in a primitive form. But you do not have to wait for physical, outer technology, for you already have the technology to heal your body by learning how to use your mind and the instrument – the technology – of your physical voice.

EXPLAINING THE SONG OF LIFE

The topic of how you manifest disease in the physical body is a complex one, which is beyond the scope of the release we give you at this point. What we give you here is an instrument for re-tuning your physical body and your three higher bodies in order to bring them into greater harmony with the Song of Life.

This Song of Life, as I hinted at before, is part of the Holy Spirit, which is created by self-aware beings transcending themselves, thereby creating an upward flow, an upward movement.

And as you might know that a river creates a sound, well so does the River of Life create a sound and it is the Song of Life. This is a rhythmic pattern that has been created over eons of time in this and previous spheres. It is a beautiful melody, not like the melodies you have on earth but nevertheless a rhythmic pattern of vibration. Of course, there are many levels of this pattern, many levels of vibration.

In the material universe, which is yet in an unascended sphere, you cannot yet fully resonate and be in complete harmony with the River of Life created in ascended spheres. But nevertheless, you do not have to be in complete synchrony with the higher spheres. You only need to use melodies that are based on the same matrix, so that they harmonize, they have the same basic rhythm, as that of the River of Life, the Song of Life.

THE CAUSE OF DISEASE

As you will know on earth, you can have a certain musical pattern where you can create many individual melodies from the same basic pattern, but they will all have a certain harmony between them. And this is exactly what you see on earth. Each physical body was, in its original, pure form, created as an individual melody that was nevertheless in harmony with the Song of Life for the earth. Since then, as we have explained, [Healing Mother Earth] various things have introduced lower manifestations, lower energies, lower rhythmic patterns that have disturbed the original harmony.

A physical body does not need to age. It does not need to become diseased. These manifestations can happen only because in your four lower bodies has been introduced mental images that, when superimposed upon the Ma-ter light, form a disharmonious rhythmic pattern, a pattern that is out of harmony with the Song of Life.

It is this disharmony that causes your cells to vibrate in a syncopated or disharmonious pattern. And therefore, they can come to a point where they cannot be maintained in the pattern that sustains the individual cells, the organs they make up, or the systems in the body, even the body itself. This then leads to aging, disease and the death of the body.

Thus, without having to know the deeper details of all of the disharmonious patterns, you can still attain much progress towards healing by using the tool we will give you to realign the rhythmic matrices of your four lower bodies with the Song of Life. And you can do this by using your physical voice to invoke the higher vibrations from the three higher levels of the material realm and from the lowest level of the spiritual realm, so that they will realign your cells.

The higher vibrations can literally accelerate, or replace, or purify the lower matrices, so that suddenly your four lower bodies are brought into greater alignment and greater harmony with the matrix based on which they were originally constructed. And this, then, is what can bring about a healing, which will bring you closer to health even though eventually you also need to see the beliefs, the ideas, the patterns that you have come to accept, so that you can undo them consciously.

RECREATING YOUR SENSE OF SELF

This, of course, is part of what will be done by the seven Chohans and the Maha Chohan in the series of books on the seven rays, the Path of the Seven Veils, the Path to Self-Mastery. But we, who are the feminine masters, desire to give you this tool, so that you can start using it as you work towards a greater conscious understanding of the seven rays and the pure qualities and the perversions of the rays, and the many subtle beliefs that underlie the perversions.

Thus, I come to give you this first installment, which truly represents the etheric or identity level. The purpose of this is to help you recreate your sense of self. And of course, we have given many teachings on this where we have explained that the core of your being is what we have called the Conscious You, which does not have what you have come to see as your individuality and personality, for it is pure awareness. It is the open door for the Presence.

Your true individuality is anchored in your I AM Presence and will be expressed from the Presence through the Conscious You. And thus, what has happened to people on earth is that they have created the outer self, what many people call the soul, and they have now come to identify themselves as the outer self so that they think that this is who they are. And if you have this sense of identity, then you must continue to project the stream of your consciousness through the matrix of that outer self.

And that, of course, means that the contents of your outer self, including the illusions that you have come to accept, will be projected upon the Ma-ter light that makes up your physical body. And thus, as long as you maintain that identification with your outer self, you simply cannot heal the conditions of your physical body, be it diseases or old age. How can you heal if you continue to do the same thing that has created the disease? This is not realistic. It is not a realistic expectation.

I know this is easy for me to say, because I am a being focused at the galactic level. And you can perhaps imagine what it is like to look at the earth from the overall view of the entire galaxy, where you see that planet earth is such a small, small planet in a large whole. Can you perhaps get some sense that when you are aware of the entire galaxy, you have a completely different perspective?

As just one visual illustration of this consider that you know that the entire galaxy moves as one whole, and there is a gravitational force that causes the entire galaxy to spin as one unit. Can you see that out of the thousands and millions and billions of stars that make up the galaxy, your planet earth is almost a microscopic speck of dust?

Even though the earth seems to have great gravity to influence your physical body, you can surely see that the gravity of the earth is as nothing compared to the total gravity of the galaxy. And thus, there is no chance that the earth can change the rotation of the galaxy. And thus, from my perspective it is very easy to say that unless you change your sense of self, you will not be able to heal your physical body.

I do realize that when you are in embodiment, this will seem infinitely more difficult. Nevertheless, I hope to give you a sense of co-measurement. I hope to help you realize that it is indeed possible to change your sense of self, and it is indeed necessary. For unless you change your sense of self, which is the highest level of your four lower bodies, how will you be able to change the lower levels, that can only work within the framework set by the higher level?

THE ROLE OF SPIRITS FOR YOUR HEALTH

Your sense of self is the framework, the basic rhythm, for the symphony of your life. Unless you make changes there, nothing can really change at the lower levels. That is why current medicine on earth has such a limited success rate, because it only seeks to make changes at the physical level by either cutting into the body or by introducing chemicals. But this is working only at the physical level and therefore does very little to change what is going on in the emotional, mental and identity levels.

You, however, do not need to be limited by the current limitations of medical technology or the medical paradigm. You can realize that you have four lower bodies and you have the potential to take command over all four of them. And when you do so, you will be able to change conditions in your physical body, for effect must follow cause.

So then, if you take what I have said here and compare it to what you have read in the book by the Maha Chohan, then you can gain another level of understanding. For I have said that every form is created by a rhythmic, vibratory pattern superimposed upon the Ma-ter light and that the form is maintained by continuously superimposing that pattern. You know, of course, that you have not consciously co-created or created your physical body. And you know that you are not consciously superimposing any matrix upon the body. So how is the matrix being superimposed upon the Ma-ter light and giving your body a continued existence? Well, it is done through what the Maha Chohan called spirits that you have created, or that you have allowed into the four levels of your mind.

There is one overall spirit, which the ascended masters have in the past called the "body elemental." And it is the spirit that is created in order to uphold the overall pattern of your physical body. But there is also an emotional elemental that upholds the overall pattern of your emotional body. And there is one for the mental body and one for the etheric or identity body.

So there are four main spirits that work together to create your physical body. It is possible that these four spirits can become so burdened by misqualified energies and imperfect beliefs that they cannot function at the optimal level. And therefore, your bodies come out of alignment with the River of Life and out of alignment with each other, and you may have diseases in any of the bodies, including mental and emotional diseases and physical diseases.

Yet how are these diseases and impure patterns introduced into your being? They are introduced by other spirits that you either create in order to deal with certain experiences on earth or that you allow to enter, such as spirits that have been created by others including the false teachers and fallen beings.

A HOUSE DIVIDED AGAINST ITSELF

When you have more than the four original spirits in your being, you have the potential for what Jesus talked about when he said that you are a house divided against yourself. There is a warring in your members, because the spirits might oppose and be at war with each other. And this, then, introduces certain disharmonious patterns from other spirits that seek to control your body spirits or seek to destroy each other. And when that war is fought within your being, then is it not obvious that you introduce all kinds of disharmonious influences, just as you see a physical war on earth can lay waste to a landscape and possibly even pollute it with radiation that lingers for many, many years after.

Again, this is not said to cause you fear. It is said to give you a realistic assessment that you have these disharmonious spirits in your being. If you have any kind of physical disease or symptoms of aging, then you should know that you have warring spirits in your four lower bodies. And again, ultimately, you will need to look at the spirits, see what was the decision that created them or allowed them to enter, and then consciously undo that decision in order to permanently dispel the spirit from your being.

This, of course, is what the Chohans will help you accomplish. But you can accomplish much by starting already and making the decision that you are willing to recreate your sense of self. You are willing to begin to contemplate this, and to ask for the help of the Chohans and the representatives of the Divine Mother to help you internalize the reality that you are not your outer personality, that you are not your ego, that you are not that separate self. You are instead the pure awareness of the Conscious You, which is meant to be an open door for the Presence.

And when you realign your sense of identity with the I AM Presence, and when you consciously decide that you are willing to let go of any aspect of the outer self in order to become more of an open door for the Presence, then something profound will happen. You will begin to realign yourself with the Presence, and that means that now the perfect matrix that the Presence holds for you and for the four lower bodies will begin to shine through your identity body. And it can then be superimposed on the mental body and eventually, as you give all of the invocations we will release, you can purify all of the four lower bodies to a large degree, and you can begin to realign them with the matrix of perfect health that is held by your I AM Presence.

RESTORING HARMONY

This in itself can either banish certain spirits from your being or diminish their influence, so that you do not reinforce them by giving them your energy. And this can then free the four elementals, the four spirits in your four lower bodies, so that they can realign themselves with the blueprint – the immaculate vision, the immaculate concept – held in your I AM Presence. This is the joy of these four spirits.

These four spirits are not evil spirits, they are not warring spirits, they are not in any way against you. They are created to serve you in your growth in self-awareness, and they may be rewarded for that service when you no longer need four lower bodies. So it is only their joy to serve you and to outpicture the matrix held in your I AM Presence, for they know that that is their reward, that is their joy, that is their highest service.

This then is a teaching that if contemplated and internalized can start the process, the alchemical process. For true alchemy is to realize exactly what I have said: That nothing in the material realm has any self-sufficient existence. It is a projection that comes through the three higher levels. And thus, the key to changing the physical is to bring all aspects of your mind, all aspects of your being, into alignment, into harmony, with your I AM Presence. That is the alchemy that will turn the base metal of the human consciousness into the gold of the Christ Consciousness. And that is the alchemy that might turn physical substances into gold, but as a beginning will turn your physical body into the highest possible state of health that will support the fulfillment of your divine plan, your sacred labor, and your spiritual mission in life.

Maraytaii, I AM. May you sometimes find time and attention to recite my name, for it realigns you with my Being. And it helps realign your identity body, your sense of self, with the cosmic reality of all life, of the upward movement of the Holy Spirit and the upward movement of the Song of Life.

Thus I say again:

Ma-ray-taii.
Ma-ray-taii.
Ma-ray-taii.

NOTE: The invocation corresponding to this chapter is: Song of Life 1 – A New Identity

The higher vibrations can literally accelerate, or replace, or purify the lower matrices, so that suddenly your four lower bodies are brought into greater alignment and greater harmony with the matrix based on which they were originally constructed.

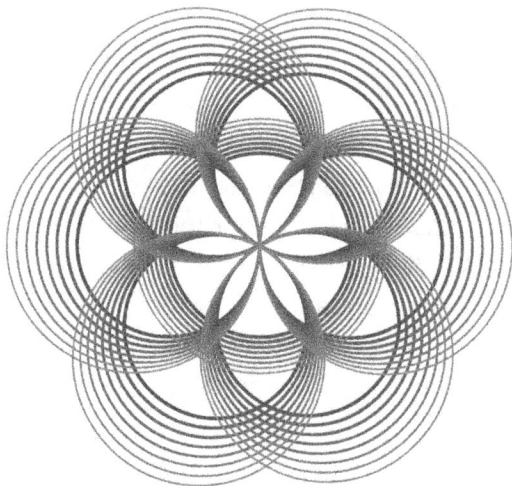

Chapter 2

USING THE MIND OR LETTING THE MIND USE YOU

Nada, I AM. I am both the Chohan of the Sixth Ray and one of the representatives of the Divine Mother for earth. I am fully capable of fulfilling both of these offices for there is, of course, no conflict between them, as there is no conflict in my own mind. And this is precisely the topic that I wish to discourse on. For you see, the cause of all disease – mental, emotional, and physical – in your being is division. Out of division springs conflict between those two parts, or more parts, who are now seen or see themselves as being in opposition to each other.

THE EARTH MOVES WITH THE GALAXY

Let me build on what Maraytaii gave you about the galactic perspective where you, from the vantage point of the center of the galaxy, can look out over the vastness of this space and see how many stars and planets there are, how they move in this beautiful coordinated movement—and then way, way down there is a little speck of dust, called planet earth. You see from the galactic perspective clearly that the earth is moving along with the gravitational fields of the entire galaxy and cannot hold up the galaxy itself.

Thus, the gravitational force, as you like to call it on earth, is indeed pulling on the earth constantly, no matter what you human beings on earth might do. You might decide, for example, that you would build giant rockets on one side of the planet and then you would fire them all so that the earth would move in the opposite direction from the direction it is being pulled by the galactic gravitational force. But no matter how many rockets you could build here on earth, you could not withstand the gravitational force of the entire galaxy. You might give yourself the illusion that you could withstand it, but in reality you could not.

Then, when you look at a galaxy and the entire material universe, you realize that the ultimate law is the Law of Free Will. The vast majority of the galaxies and the vast majority of the planets with intelligent life have all chosen to move upward in the upward, ascending spiral that we have called the River of Life and the Holy Spirit. These untold billions of self-aware beings have chosen to unite their minds – their individual minds – in this giant flow of the collective, upward-flowing mind.

Yet because of the Law of Free Will, there are certain planets in the cosmos where the majority of the inhabitants have chosen not to join in with the River of Life, the upward flow. Earth is, of course, one of these planets. And that is why you see so many conditions on this earth that are unbalanced, including conditions in nature where you have lack and natural disasters. Also, conditions in the physical bodies of human beings where you have fatigue and various forms of disease, be they physical or mental.

THE DIVISION OF OPPOSING SPIRITS

You see, then, that the cause of all disease is that there is a division in your being, which means that there are two divisions that are working against each other. This can happen at many different levels. Of course, there are the four levels we have talked about: the identity, mental, emotional and physical. But there are even different levels. For it is possible for you to have spirits that are designed to do one particular thing for you but then you have another spirit that works against it.

As an example of this, you have the fact that many people have from past lives created certain spirits that are selfish, self-centered, perhaps have a tendency to become angry in certain situations. But then, in later lifetimes, these people have adopted a religious or even a spiritual outlook on life. And now they have decided that it is not right, or spiritual, or Christian, or Buddhist to be angry. But rather than looking at their own minds, discovering the spirit that caused them to set up a pattern of reacting with anger in the first place, they have instead created another spirit which is designed to suppress the angry spirit. You now have these two spirits that are designed for opposite purposes, and they are from the very beginning at war with each other.

Often people are not aware of this war because in some cases spiritual people are actually so good at allowing the one spirit to suppress their anger that the anger rarely reaches the conscious mind. Yet I can assure you that no spirit created in the material realm can ultimately defeat another. You may have an angry spirit. You may have created a spirit to suppress the angry spirit. But the suppressing spirit cannot destroy the angry spirit. It does not have the power to do so. Why does it not have the power? Because it is not self-aware.

You created the angry spirit. The pure awareness that you are, the Conscious You that you are, you created the angry spirit. You created the suppressing spirit. And only you, who have created these spirits, can uncreate them, can dissolve them, can let them go.

My point here is this: The suppressing spirit may be so powerful in suppressing the angry spirit that you do not realize you are angry. You do not realize you have the angry spirit. Yet this angry spirit is still residing in your emotional body. There may be a component of it in the mental body and even in the identity realm. You think it is justified that life should live up to certain expectations and if it does not, then it is acceptable for you to become angry, for this is not the way life is supposed to be.

SUBCONSCIOUS PROJECTIONS

You see now that the spirits in the higher levels are beyond your conscious awareness because the suppressing spirit is not neutralizing the other spirits but it is neutralizing your conscious awareness of them. It is suppressing the spirits only at the conscious level, but they are still active at the higher levels. This means you are still projecting images and energy through those spirits into the cosmic mirror. And that is why the cosmic mirror can only mirror back to you exactly what you are sending out.

The fallacy of many of the teachings that are out there on self-help is that they promise you that you can gain tremendous results by changing your conscious attitude and adopting a "positive mental attitude." But it simply is not correct, my beloved. For unless you come to the point where you see the spirits at the higher levels, and where you consciously dissolve them, then you will simply create another spirit, a "positive mental attitude spirit" which might manage eventually – when you feed it enough energy – to suppress the other spirits at the conscious level only.

Thus, you think at the conscious level: "I am so positive, all I am sending out is positive energy, therefore the cosmic mirror should give me back positive circumstances." And when you do not get back positive circumstances, you get discouraged and think something must be wrong. But what you do not realize is that the cosmic mirror does not mirror back only what is at your conscious level; it mirrors back the totality of what you are projecting out with your four lower bodies.

You see now that what I am getting at here is something very simple: You cannot withstand the collective pull of the mind, the collective mind, created on earth. You cannot personally withstand this. You can try to create spirits that will suppress the collective mind and its tendencies towards anger or aggression or what have you, but you will not be successful. Except maybe at the conscious level, so that you fool yourself into thinking you are such a spiritual, such a kind, such a loving person. But you will still be affected by the spirits at the higher levels of your mind, which are beneath the level of conscious awareness, in what is normally called the subconscious mind.

SEEKING TO CONTROL THOUGHTS

What do you see in many spiritual people, even in many people who have been very sincere for many years and have meditated? What you see is this: They have realized that part of what they need to do in order to grow spiritually is to control the mind, to avoid certain disturbing thoughts or even perhaps to avoid all thoughts. So what have they done? They have created a spirit that seeks to control their thoughts, that seeks to suppress either certain thoughts or all thoughts.

Now, there are several things that are not constructive about this approach. First of all, it is impossible to do except at the conscious level. You might actually be successful in suppressing thoughts at the conscious level, so that you think you can go into deep meditation and you do not have any thoughts. But that does not necessarily mean that you have cleared your higher bodies. Some people have been successful, through meditation and other spiritual practices, at clearing their higher bodies. But they have been successful only for one reason: They have been willing to look at everything that has been going on in those bodies and dismiss it. These are those who are successful in applying a spiritual teaching, whatever that teaching may be.

But there are many people, especially in the modern western world, who take a more superficial approach and think it is all a matter of producing a certain effect—and they are not willing to go into the depths of the mind. They are so focused on producing an effect, and because they are so focused on producing an effect – whether it be to still the mind or something else – they create a spirit that is meant to produce that effect. As I have said, the spirit can do this at the conscious level, but the spirit cannot resolve the spirits at the deeper levels.

You have many people who have the illusion they are spiritual but they are not, for they have not resolved what is going on at the deeper levels. My point here is simply this: Part of the Song of Life, the part that I am introducing, is the mental level. Maraytaii talked about the identity level and I am talking about the mental. Many people believe that in order to control their mental body, they somehow have to control their thoughts— either direct them into following certain patterns or still them altogether by suppressing all thoughts.

THE MENTAL CAUSE OF DISEASE

However, as I have attempted to explain, this will inevitably create a division in your being where you will create several spirits that are at war with each other. This will eat up your energy. The warring in the members will also create this division that over time will manifest as disease in the physical body.

Because what is the physical body? It is a projection of the mind. Everything is mind. Your physical body does not exist in some physical space, as you have been brought up to believe based on the current scientific understanding of the universe—which is still so tied to your physical senses.

The deeper reality is, as Maraytaii is saying, that everything is being re-created many times a second. Your body does not exist over time. It is constantly being re-created by an image being projected onto the Ma-ter light. That image is being projected through the three higher levels of your three higher bodies and even through the mind at the physical level.

When you have a division in the mental level, for example, it will eventually filter through to the physical. You will now have an imperfect image, an image with contradictions, being projected onto the Ma-ter light. And this will manifest as some kind of warring in the physical body where the cells cannot function correctly and maybe even destroy themselves or destroy other cells, so that you eventually have a disease that destroys an organ or a body part or even causes the entire body to break down. It cannot be any other way, for the physical body can only outpicture what is being projected from the other levels.

What I am saying here is simply this: If you think that taking control of the mind means stilling all thoughts, then this is not a constructive approach. What we propose to do in this healing method of the Song of Life is to give you an alternative where you do not seek to suppress thoughts. You do not seek to control thoughts. You actually allow the thoughts to flow.

For the simple reason is this: You cannot change anything from the past. You cannot go back in time and make changes in the past. You can only make changes in the now, in the present. What the mental mind does is it projects a mental image and then it projects that this mental image is not an image; it is reality.

Now, in a sense there is some truth to this because, as I have said, the mental images are projected onto the Ma-ter light and therefore become your temporary reality. But they are not reality in the ultimate sense. They are concepts. They are mental images.

CHANGING MENTAL IMAGES

What you need to do, in order to make changes at the physical level, is change the mental images. But here is the key. You cannot change the mental images in the past. You can only change them in the now. And you can only do this by using your creative abilities.

You cannot actually destroy a mental image. This is not constructive to even attempt. But this is what the mind tells you that you must do, because the separate mind has become trapped in the dualistic form of thinking, and in the dualistic form of thinking the basic polarities of the expanding force of the Father and the contracting force of the Mother are now seen as opposites. The separate mind, the serpentine mind, attaches a value judgment, saying that one is good and one is evil. Therefore, one must be destroyed so that good can prevail.

But you see, these dualistic polarities are created at the same time and they are co-dependent. They cannot exist without the other. If you destroyed evil as you define it, good would seize to exist. And therefore, you can never destroy evil by using the dualistic mind.

But what the mind does – what the mental mind is good at – is using the intellectual faculty of analyzing, comparing, and creating a system that says: "These thoughts are good, these thoughts are bad. I must find a way to destroy the bad thoughts." What the mind says, which is its real expertise, is: "There is a problem I must solve before I can be healthy or before I can be spiritual. And that problem involves that something has gone wrong and I must go in and correct the wrong by destroying what was wrong."

Now, you are trapped in the game where you seek to identify and uncover a mental matrix that supposedly is wrong. And then you seek to destroy that mental matrix. But what are you doing? Exactly what I described earlier. There may be a mental matrix that is not constructive and that mental matrix has now turned into a spirit and the spirit is constantly projecting that matrix. But if you use the mind to seek to deal with this problem, you will simply create another spirit that is designed to try to destroy the old one. As I have said, this does not lead to resolution. Healing does not mean what you have come to believe here on earth where you think that if a cell has cancer, you need to destroy that cell.

CREATIVE HEALING

You cannot heal through destruction, my beloved. Would you please consider this one simple statement and allow it to be absorbed in your being. For if you want to attain healing and wholeness, you must realize you cannot heal by destroying. You leave wholeness through division. You cannot return to wholeness by having one division attempt to destroy another division. This will only accelerate your descent away from wholeness.

What must you do? You must re-activate the mind's ability to be creative. Creativity is not that you seek to identify a problem and destroy that problem. Creativity is when you say: "Ah, this old matrix does not work for me anymore. I do not want it anymore. I am looking for a higher matrix. I am transcending the old matrix. I am re-creating my sense of self. I am re-creating my mental body and my thoughts." Do you see?

By being creative you transcend the old. You do not destroy the old. How do you overcome, for example, cancer? Not by seeking to destroy the cells that are outpicturing the cancer, for this only adds to the force of division and self-destruction and warring in the members. You do so by loving the cells. You do so by looking beyond the outer, physical conflict to the emotional, the mental, and the identity component that has caused you to project these images upon the cells that are now causing the cells to self-destruct and to destroy others.

Do you see? It is through creativity that you transcend the divided matrices that cause disease and conflict. But creativity is love: love for that which is more, love for that which is new, love for that which transcends the old.

THE CHOICE OF ATTUNEMENT

Do you see what I am seeking to say here? You, as a human being on earth, have a choice: To which mind, to which collective mind, do you want to attune your individual mind? Do you want to attune it to the collective mind created here on earth, or do you want to attune it to the greater collective mind created in the entire universe?

The greater collective mind – the Holy Spirit, the River of Life – is an upward-going creative mind. The collective mind created on earth is a divided mind where there is warring in the members—which you see outpictured as groups of people constantly seeking to destroy each other.

As long as you are attuned to that mind, you will not find it very easy to find healing. Certainly, you will not find wholeness. You may cover over physical symptoms for a time but you will only cover it over. You will not truly heal it, you will not resolve it.

What we are offering you through this tool of the Song of Life is a way to clear the levels of your mind and therefore begin to attune your individual mind to the greater mind, to the River of Life. We do this by giving you this tool where you can use the power of your voice, the spoken word, to invoke spiritual light, to invoke the sound patterns of the Song of Life. This will begin to realign the repetitive patterns produced in your four lower bodies and projected onto the Ma-ter light that makes up your physical body.

This is a different approach to healing. It is a viable approach to healing. It may not be instantaneous, but then again, if you can shift your mind enough, it can be instantaneous healing. For the moment your mind has shifted to the point where you are no longer projecting the patterns that cause the disease in your physical body, well, at that moment your physical body can be re-created instantly.

Is that not the logical consequence of the teaching we have given you that everything in the material world is being projected upon the Ma-ter light many times a second? Do you not, then, see that once you change the matrix, the physical manifestation will change instantly?

This is what Jesus knew when he healed the man with the withered arm, when he performed other healings, so-called miracles. They were not miracles at all. He was able to use his attainment to help the people overcome the matrix – shift out of the matrix – that they had projected upon the physical body. That is why he asked them: "Believest thou that I have the power to do this?" And when they believed, then they could be healed.

Now, some of them, I must tell you – even though it is not recorded in the Bible – lapsed back, and after some time they went back into their old disease because they were not able to build upon the grace given to them by Christ and consciously re-create their sense of self. Therefore, after a short period of time, they recreated the same pattern that again projected the disease back onto their physical bodies.

Nevertheless, I am telling you the reality, which is the Christ reality. The Christ in you has the power to bring about instantaneous healing of your physical body, of your emotional body, of your mental body, of your identity body.

"Believest thou this?" For then it shall be done onto you as thou believest. This is the Law of Free Will, my beloved. It is not wishful thinking. It is the law.

THE CHALLENGE OF BELIEF

However, saying to someone: "You should believe this" is of course not very constructive. Many cannot believe it because they have too much baggage in the four levels of the mind. They have too much misqualified energy. They have too many dualistic beliefs. And that is why, even though I want you to know this reality, I do not want you to feel bad if you cannot instantly believe.

But yet I know that some can instantly believe and can instantly change. And I certainly want that option to be open for those who can take advantage of it. But for those who cannot, use the tools we have given you. Not only the Song of Life, but the many other tools we have given: decrees, invocations, teachings that you study – especially the teachings from the Seven Chohans – and then work on shifting your sense of self. For are you not beginning to realize, even by listening to this and by giving these invocations of the Song of Life, that you can shift your sense of self and that you are the only one who can do so?

The Christ cannot shift your self for you. Only the Conscious You can shift its sense of self. But the Christ can help you facilitate that shift when you make the decision to let go of the old. You are the only one who can let go because you have free will. You are the only one who can use your ability – the ability of returning to pure awareness – so that you can look at your mental body from the outside and say: "Ah, I see what the mind is doing. I see that my mind is like a computer. It has been programmed to execute certain functions and it will keep doing so mindlessly for the indefinite future, unless I pick up the mouse and click somewhere else or say quit to the program that has been going on now for lifetimes in my mental body. I see now that the mind is programmed to solve certain problems. But I see that I, the Conscious You, do not need to solve these problems. They do not need to be solved. They need to be transcended. They need to be left behind."

This is the key to healing: That you shift your sense of self at the identity level, at the mental level, the emotional level, and at the physical. Believest thou that you have the power to do this? Then you can be helped by the Song of Life and by the teachings of the ascended masters. If you do not believe that you have the power to change your sense of self, then we cannot help you, I regret to say.

You must then join the School of Hard Knocks until you have had so many hard knocks that you become open to saying: "There must be a better way than this." Then, you can begin to ask yourself where the knocks come from—and they come from the divisions in your own being. You can realize that you have created those divisions, and while this may be hard to realize at first, the beauty of it is, my beloved, that what you have created you also have the power to uncreate.

Believest thou this? Then embrace the tools we have given you. Embrace the teachings and shift your sense of identity. Shift out of the mind that thinks it has to do all these things, that thinks it has to solve all of these problems, that thinks it needs to save other people or save the planet. Instead, focus on saving yourself by returning to pure awareness. Thus, use the Song of Life but do not think that one tool can do it all for you, for it will not happen automatically.

Believest thou this? Then receive an impetus of joy, an impetus of love, an impetus of healing from the heart of Nada, the Chohan of the Sixth Ray and a representative of the Divine Mother. For that I AM, healing I AM, wholeness I AM, peace of mind I AM. Believest thou this? For only then will I be so for you.

NOTE: The invocation corresponding to this chapter is:
Song of Life 2 – A New Mind

Chapter 3

LETTING FEELINGS FLOW

Kuan Yin is the name I have used for a long time in my service to earth. I have been known primarily in the East. Yet, I have long since attained the consciousness of Buddhahood. And when you do attain Buddhahood, you do so by transcending all labels that can be put upon one on earth.

Thus, even the very concept that there is a so-called religion of Buddhism and that this has some kind of monopoly on the Buddha and his teachings is a misnomer. For truly, when you attain the level of Buddhic consciousness, you become completely and utterly universal. You go beyond all labels on earth.

This is indeed symbolized in the story, which has been told many times in different versions, that I have a Prajna boat, a so-called wisdom boat, whereby I can take people across the raging Sea of Samsara. But why is the Sea of Samsara raging? Because it is churned up by the turbulent emotions of humankind, the turbulent emotional energies that have been stored in the collective energy field, the collective consciousness, for a very long time.

NAVIGATING THE SEA OF EMOTIONS

Thus, what is it you need in order to navigate this raging sea? You need the wisdom that enables you to neither go into this extreme nor into that extreme so that you stay on an even keel. You keep the boat on a steady course even though you sometimes navigate around raging waves coming against you. But you do not seek to fight them, nor do you submit to them and let them drift your boat. You keep your eye on the prize. You keep your eye on the farther shore, and you keep steering in the shortest way towards that shore where you follow the principle followed by water of going around any obstacle, so you gently flow through the raging waves. This is how the effervescent wisdom of the Buddha guides you to always find the Middle Way between extremes.

The Middle Way is to avoid the one opposite extreme, which we might symbolize by ice that is frozen. The Middle Way is to avoid the other opposite extreme, which we might symbolize by melting and melted lava that keeps boiling and bubbling at great heat. Yet the Middle Way is also avoiding the midpoint between these two extremes, which is indifference.

For the Buddha, of course, in his own time, was precisely met with indifference from most people. They were, in many cases, so completely convinced and preoccupied with the religion of Hinduism that they had but indifference towards this Buddha who claimed to have some new kind of wisdom that was beyond that of the Hindu brahmins. This is also why you saw many people ignore Jesus in his time and why you see people ignore the ascended masters today. Even though I can assure you that the fact that we can speak directly, in these worded dictations, through messengers in embodiment is indeed one of the major forces of renewal in the religious landscape of this planet.

TAKING ON A ROLE

Let us take a look at the emotional body of man and woman. We have explained to you that you have four lower bodies. The highest of these is the identity body and then comes the mental and the third body is the emotional.

You need to understand that in the emotional body it is very easy to be pulled in different directions by two, often opposing, forces. Yet, in many cases, the forces are not perhaps as opposing as it might feel since they are in the end pulling you in the same direction.

Now, it is not the intention of us, who are the representatives of the Divine Mother, to go deeply into the existence of beings on earth who seek to control humankind. We have done so elsewhere, especially in our book, *Healing Mother Earth,* which you might find occasion to study if you are interested in more about this topic. Yet it is absolutely necessary for your personal healing and growth to realize that there are forces embodied and not embodied that are seeking to control you, and they do so by seeking to control all of your four lower bodies.

Thus, of course, you have the teaching that in order to even take embodiment, as explained by the Maha Chohan *[Flowing with the River of Life],* you need to start out by creating some kind of spirit that can integrate with the physical body. Those who are the manipulators of humankind have been very good at creating these predefined roles for what it means to be a human being in embodiment on earth. These roles then exist as spirits in the identity level of the planet, the identity level of the collective consciousness.

Many beings who have taken embodiment for the first time on earth, whether it was their first embodiment or whether they descended here from a different place, have chosen to take on one of these predefined roles almost as if they walked into an earthly theater, looked at the different costumes that were hanging on the racks, looked at the roles and what they would outplay and said: "I want to try what it would be like to be that one."

BEING CONTROLLED BY YOUR ROLE

You take on a role that would define you as a human being and defines what you can, and especially what you cannot, do as a human being. But you have taken on this role. This then sets the stage, sets the pattern. For of course, you will know that in a theater on earth you have a predefined script and all actors who take part in the play must follow the script, must they not? There is no room for spontaneity. There is no room for throwing away the script and making up your own way, for this will confuse the other players and the audience and those who think they run the theater.

Yet, of course, if you take on a predefined role at the identity level, that role will set certain limitations for what can happen in your thought body, in your mental body, and that again will set limitations for what can happen in your feeling body, which again sets limitations for what you can do with the physical body.

So do you see, if you look back at history, that many societies have had a clearly elitist tendency? Have you ever asked yourself the question of why so many of the societies seen in history have been ruled by a small elite where the general population have been either the direct slaves or at least the indirect slaves, working to keep the elite in their privileged position or to in other ways do the bidding of the elite, such as go to war against another group of elitist beings in another country? Why is this so? Have you ever asked yourself this question?

It is indeed so because most of the lifestreams that currently embody on earth have chosen to take on these predefined roles that were defined in the identity realm by those who seek to control humankind. What does this mean: to control humankind? Well, it means that you control what people will do in the physical so that most of the time you can keep the general population pacified, you can keep them in indifference.

But at certain times, you can have them go towards either one extreme or the other. One extreme being that they are so riled up by anger or hatred against another group that they are willing to do whatever they want to defeat that group in a war. This is what you have seen in many wars on earth. But it can also be the other extreme of being so cold, so insensitive to life, that you are willing to kill even civilians – even those who have not attacked you – because you have become so numb and insensitive that you no longer see them as human beings. This is what you have seen in many atrocities against human populations seen throughout the ages.

THE THREE EMOTIONAL REACTIONS

You see, those who are the manipulators accomplish this by setting a pattern in the identity realm, by setting other patterns for what you think about by defining these predefined philosophies and ideologies, and also by setting certain patterns for how you react emotionally. They have attempted to get people to go into one of these three emotional reactions that I have described.

One is that your emotional body is completely frozen so you suppress, or think you have to suppress, all emotions so that you do not feel anything at all. Look at how many places in society this is encouraged. For example, in the business world there are many people who are brought up to never show any emotion no matter what their supervisors do or say. But this is the only way to get success in the business world in many cases. Of course, it is the same with many other organizations where you must go along to get along by never objecting, by never speaking out, by never saying: "This just isn't right" or "This just doesn't feel right."

Then, on the other hand, see how they also want other people to go into the reaction where their emotional bodies are like bubbling lava where they are constantly agitated, constantly angry, so that at the slightest agitation they will suddenly burst out into anger, such as where you, for example, see uprisings in various countries. And also as you see at certain sporting events every Saturday or Sunday.

Yet, of course, you also see many people who are in the middle – but not in the Middle Way – where they are almost indifferent to anything that happens, so that it takes a very big provocation to even stir them into feeling anything, any sense of responsibility, for what is going on in their society.

YOU CANNOT IGNORE EMOTIONS

Do you see what I am getting at with this teaching? When it comes to your personal healing, which of course is the main topic of this Song of Life matrix, your emotions are very important, for the emotional body is right above the physical body. Not only is it the emotions that are directly projected onto the Mat-ter light in the physical spectrum – and therefore your emotions are the very matrices that are determining the physical characteristics of your body – but on top of that your emotions are also the key to your healing.

Do you see, if you look at society and the three reactions I described earlier: You have many, many people who have come to the point where they see the danger of letting their emotions turn into bubbling lava. They see the dangers of letting you become so cold and insensitive to the suffering of others that you stand by while the holocaust is taking place in your backyard. As a result, there are many people in today's world who do not want to deal with emotion.

This is, of course, partly because they have grown up to think that their emotions can only be locked into one of these reactions, and they have not been taught how to deal with their emotions in a more constructive manner. They have been brought up to think that emotions are something that are kind of like the slave of whatever events happen in your life. If certain events happen in your life, then you can only feel that way about it. And since it does not seem like you can take control over the external events that happen in your life, it seems like you cannot take control over your emotions.

Well, of course, people have not been taught that the emotions are set on a track by the mental and the identity. Do you see the result? Many people in today's world do not want to deal with emotions. They would rather ignore them. But do you not see, my beloved, that if you have a physical disease, or fatigue, or aging in your physical body, then you cannot hope to heal this without working with the emotional body (and of course the mental and identity bodies)?

But do you see that you cannot skip the emotional, as many people in the modern world want to do, and go directly to the mental and identity levels? Do you not see that there are many people in the world who have become so intellectual in their approach to life that they think that all they need to do is sit around and analyze everything, including their own lives, for they think that the analytical mind can come up with answers to all problems? Or there are even those who go into more of the identity level of looking into philosophical, or religious, or spiritual teachings, seeking for answers there.

I am not saying it is not valid to look for answers in the mental and identity realms. I am only saying that if you do so and ignore the emotions, want to skip the emotions, how can you attain healing in the physical?

THE EMOTIONS ARE THE KEY TO HEALING

Do you not see that you may sit at the mental and identity levels and build a perfect thought matrix, for example, for the health of your physical body, but how will you get that matrix transferred to the physical level? It can happen in only one way: through the emotional body. You cannot project with the analytical mind a thought matrix directly onto the Ma-ter light. It cannot be done, my beloved. And that is why you will see many people who are so trapped in their intellectual pursuits that they think they can solve all of the world's problems intellectually, but in reality they have very little impact on the physical realm. They are so out of touch, so in denial of their emotions, that they cannot transfer their mental ideas to the physical level. That transfer can happen only through the intermediary level of the emotional.

Thus, you see many people become physically ill and before they became ill they thought they could live life a certain way, often based on a certain intellectual understanding or philosophy. They were simply living their lives ignoring the need to deal with their emotions, whether their emotions were hot or cold or indifferent. And then they become ill physically and they realize they need to do something about their life, they have to change something in their life, but they still think they can find an analytical solution, whether it be to come up with this or that chemical or surgical procedure, or diet, or some kind of alternative physical exercise to take care of the body.

Yet, even though some healing – or at least some masking of symptoms – can happen at the physical level, the natural, the holistic, the higher way of attaining healing is to also deal with the emotional body. Truly, why have we started out talking about the identity and the mental body? Because once you do shift your sense of identity and shift out of the analytical mind, then it does become much easier for you to deal with the emotional body.

Once you have learned to use your voice to invoke spiritual energy and get that spiritual energy flowing more freely through your identity and mental bodies, it becomes much easier to have that energy flow into the emotional body where it can begin to consume the stored emotional energies and thereby also clear out and purify your emotional body. Yet, what I seek to point out to you here is this: You will not attain ultimate success unless you shift your approach to the point where you are now willing to directly look at your emotional body and to directly look at the feelings you have there. This is what I will give you some pointers for doing in this discourse.

YOUR EMOTIONS ARE NOT YOURS

As I said, many people have been brought up to think there is nothing they can do about emotions and that they need to suppress whatever disturbing emotions come up. As we have explained, what is it that happens? Well, your emotions are not *your* emotions.

As the Maha Chohan has explained, all of your negative, inharmonious emotions come from spirits. You, meaning the pure awareness of the Conscious You, are not feeling these emotions.

It is the spirits that are producing the emotions and you are only experiencing them because you are experiencing life through the filter of the spirits. They are not your emotions. But how, my beloved, will you ever see this unless you look at the emotional body, unless you look at the emotion? And how will you ever look at the emotions if you attempt to suppress them or ignore them?

There is only one way to see that these feelings are not yours, and that is to stop running away from your feelings and instead reverse direction and run directly into your feelings until you stand inside that raging volcano, or until you stand there on that cold ice sheet of the cold, frozen emotion. Only when you get in touch with the emotion and then go through the emotion, will you be able to see that the emotion is not who you are. It is not even how you feel.

Nor is it even a product of certain thoughts that have set a pattern for your reaction to the circumstances on earth, for the thoughts also come from spirits if they are lower, self-centered thoughts based on the fear of separation. Neither are you really that identity who feels like a limited human being who is trapped in a cage and can only lash out when someone rattles the cage. You are pure awareness. But how will you know this until you experience pure awareness?

You may say that pure awareness is experienced when you project yourself to the identity level, which is the open door between the spiritual and the four realms of the material world. But how will you get to the identity level unless you go through the emotions, my beloved? For when you are in a physical body, your conscious awareness is centered at the physical level. You have the ability, as we have said, to project yourself anywhere you want to go, but you cannot project yourself directly into the identity body. Well, you can in theory, but for most people this is not possible because they will be pulled into the emotional body when they attempt to go beyond the physical.

For the vast majority of people, it is not possible for them to go directly into the identity. So how will they get there and experience pure awareness? Only by first going into the emotional body, going into the emotions until you go through the emotions, then into the mental body, then go into the thoughts until you go through the thoughts, then go into the identity, then go through the sense of self until you experience pure awareness. This is what can happen for all people who are willing to follow the process and to keep applying it.

There are, of course, some people who can go directly to the identity level or the spiritual level, but that is because they have, at some point in their past, cleaned up their emotional body so that it does not pull them into these reactions.

IDENTIFYING WITH EMOTIONS

What we attempt to do here is to help you develop the ability and the willingness to go into the emotion, to get in touch with your emotions and to go through them. We know that in the beginning this can be scary, but that is why we have given you these exercises that you can do for invoking spiritual light. For as you do this and continue to do this over time, you will invoke light that will start to clear out some of the accumulated energy that makes your emotional body either a frozen wasteland or a raging volcano. And when the intensity of the emotions is taken down a few notches, then it becomes much easier for you to go into them.

Yet, of course, we know that even so this can be scary for many people who are not used to doing this, and so we offer that for each one of you we are willing to take you by the hand

and take you through the process. We will offer you that you can go to the etheric retreat that we maintain, we the ascended masters, the representatives of the Divine Mother. You can come and learn so that when you come to the point of doing this at the conscious level, you are familiar with the process. You know what it feels like. You know it is not nearly as bad as it might seem. You know that you can survive going into the inferno of the emotions, for you will not be burned. You will not be burned. Neither will you be frozen and paralyzed. The deeper reality that we teach you is that the emotions are the key to your physical healing. Why is this?

Have we not said that when you start at the identity level, you are dealing with something that is very ethereal, meaning that it is easy to change? Once you are at the identity level, it is fairly ease to change your identity. Then, when you go down to the mental level, your sense of identity has set a certain limitation for how many options you can see at the mental level, and this sets limitations for where your thoughts can go. Just look at how many people in the world have decided that a particular religion must provide the highest truth, so in their attempts to find answers they dare do not go beyond the doctrines and dogmas of that religion. Or look at how other people have decided that materialism provides the ultimate truth and thus they dare not ask for answers beyond the framework set by a materialistic outlook on life. The same, of course, for political ideology.

Yet when you go to the emotional level – and this is one of the reasons why people are scared of emotions – you have something that is more concrete than thoughts. Once your emotions are locked on a track, such as anger – once you have crossed that threshold of becoming angry – then you know it is far more difficult to pull yourself out of the anger. And do you see why that is?

Think about how people talk about their feelings: "I am angry. I became angry. He was angry." Do you see what has happened here? When you say, "I am," you are using a statement that belongs at the identity level, but you have pulled it down to the emotional level, and now you think you are anger. You are angry. You are an angry person.

You may even say about people that they are angry people because most of the time they are angry, they respond with anger. It is their default emotion, just as other people have other emotions as their default reaction to life. This is what, of course, makes it so difficult for people to change their emotions because they are identified with them. If you can say "I feel angry" – meaning, I am a separate "I" feeling angry – it is much easier for you to step outside the feeling. But when you identify yourself as "I am angry," how can you step outside that feeling? It is far more difficult.

TAKING RESPONSIBILITY FOR FEELINGS

Feelings are harder to change than thoughts. And of course, as most of you have experienced, the physical level, including your physical bodies after they become ill, are harder to change than feelings. But what I am saying here is that you cannot change the physical body if you do not change your feelings.

The all-important understanding you need to attain here is that feelings can be changed only when you take responsibility. And taking responsibility for your feelings means that first of all you do not run away from them. You do not ignore them. You acknowledge that these feelings exist. But the other aspect of taking responsibility is that you go into them until you stand inside the feeling and experience that the emotional energy is around you but you are not the emotional energy.

Do you see that it might seem counterintuitive that taking responsibility for your feelings involves actually realizing they are not yours? But this is the consequence of going into them and experiencing that they are just energy whirling around. They really have no long-term significance for feelings are, as we have said before, energy in motion, e-motion.

When you identify with them, when you say: "I am angry," then you think they have some kind of long-term, universal, or cosmic significance. You think, when your anger becomes intense enough, that you have to act on the anger because there must be a change, there must be some physical result that has to be manifest. In other words, once you cross that threshold of seeing "I am angry," then you also automatically step into thinking and feeling that you must act on the anger. You must express it. It must be expressed at the physical level as some form of action.

YOU DO NOT NEED TO ACT ON EMOTION

But when you look at the emotion, go right into it, and you stand inside this ball of swirling emotion, you see that inside of it is just emptiness. In fact, when you come to a certain point, you will see that inside the energy in motion there is stillness, as if you were standing in the nucleus of an atom watching how the electrons are swirling around it. And that is when you can experience directly, intuitively – you can have the gnosis of experiencing – that emotional energy is just energy. It has no cosmic, or epic or long-term significance. It does not need to be acted upon. It does not need to be taken out into physical action.

My beloved, when you begin to experience this, several things can happen. You can come to the point where you no longer allow your negative emotions to be projected onto the cells of your physical body. Therefore, you can free the cells of the body from this constant projection of negative emotional energy that has caused those cells to manifest a physical disease. And this of course is the key to physical healing, for as we have said, everything is a projection of mental images.

There is a projection – a certain matrix of identity – that exists in your identity body. When the light from your spiritual self, your I AM Presence, flows through the identity body, it takes on the form of that matrix. It is as if you have a movie projector projecting that image onto the mental body. But then another image exists in the mental body and that image is projected into the emotions where again it is changed by what is in your emotional body. And then the final image is projected onto the cells of your physical body.

How will you attain healing of a physical disease that is caused by this projection from the emotional body, unless you change the projection? And how will you change the projection unless you go into the emotion and see that it does not need to be acted upon? It is just energy whirling around and you can, in fact, transform, consume, and raise to a higher vibration the energy at the emotional level before it flows into the physical.

Doing this is precisely what you can do by using the tools we have given you of these invocations. When you read them out loud at the physical level, you are not only at the physical, you are reaching into your emotional, mental and identity bodies. You are reaching beyond the physical to other realms.

Do you see that what we are seeking to do here is to free up all aspects of your being so that you can flow with the River of Life? But do you see that as long as your emotional body is frozen, well obviously there is no flow, is there? But even when your emotional body is a raging volcano there is no flow either because a bubbling volcano is so uncoordinated that it is just a matter of chance how it flows towards the ocean. There is no constructive direction in that flow, and that is why you see so many people get themselves into progressively difficult situations until they have a full-blown crises and they are so paralyzed that they do not know what do to.

THE ONLY WAY OUT IS TO FLOW

What we seek to do for you here is give you a vision that you are here for a purpose, that you came to earth for a purpose. You did not come to earth simply to have negative emotions, to feel bad about life, to feel that life is not living up to your expectations and to spend an entire lifetime being frustrated because life is not what you think it should be and therefore you are constantly in an agitated emotional state. Or you have shut down your emotions to the point where you expect nothing from life, where you think that life is something that has to be endured until you are done and out of here. But you will not be out of here until you flow out of here with the River of Life. There is no escape from physical embodiment. You will re-embody again and again in progressively more difficult situations until you learn to use your co-creative abilities to flow with the River of Life so that you can co-create your way out of here instead of expecting some external savior to do it for you.

Of course, there is an external savior and it is the River of Life. When you attune your mind and your feelings to that River of Life, you will begin to flow. Life will begin to flow. The frozen emotions begin to melt like you see the ice melting in the spring, and suddenly a frozen river begins to crack and then the ice fractures and the water starts moving downstream. And it warms up and it melts and suddenly there are open patches in the river and it starts flowing faster until it reaches the ocean. And the river is here and spring is here.

Or you see even a bubbling volcano that suddenly finds an outlet so that it begins to flow and yet as it flows it cools, and then suddenly you are free from these patterns of going from one negative emotion to another and going from one agitated situation to another. And your life is now free to flow, flow in new directions so that you can change something.

For I am sure that you are familiar with the famous quote by Albert Einstein where he said that if you keep doing the same thing and expect different results, you are insane. And indeed, he was pointing out a universal principle. As long as you have the same identity matrices projected into your mental body, the same mental matrices projected into your emotional body, and the same emotional matrices projected onto the cells and atoms of your physical body, then nothing can change.

The disease manifest in your physical body cannot change, for it is a projection from the three higher bodies. Thus, if you want to escape the insanity, you must do something different. And that means you must learn to get your emotions to flow in an upward direction rather than being either frozen or caught in these repetitive patterns of agitation.

THREE PRIMARY EMOTIONS

There are two primary emotions that drive the emotional bodies of most people. One is fear, which paralyzes and freezes you. The other is anger, which agitates you. And then the third primary emotion is what we might call indifference, where you are not actually frozen nor are you hot and bubbling, but you are simply refusing to be aware. You are refusing to use your self-awareness to be aware of your surroundings, to be aware of yourself and your potential to change.

When you are frozen, you cannot see how to change. When you are bubbling hot you cannot see how to change. When you are indifferent you can see how to change but you will not. So you continue to react to life without admitting that you do not have to continue to react the same way, for you can change something.

This, then, is the beauty of the invocation to the emotional body. When you give it, it will begin to change your emotions. It will begin to help them flow. And when you make conscious decisions to make them flow, to go into them – to go into the negative ones and to reach for the positive feelings – then change will begin to happen.

How far this change will go is up to you, for no invocation can go against your free will. But if you will ask us, whichever one of the feminine masters is closest to your heart, then we will help you come to the point where you can decide to just let the emotions flow. And I can assure you that when you begin to let the emotions flow while giving our invocations, all of them, your emotions will, after an initial period where they simply need to be expressed so as to reinstate the movement, they will begin to take on a direction, and it will be an upward, positive direction. And as your emotions begin to shift towards that higher level, then you will not have negative emotions projected onto the cells of your physical body. You will now have positive ones.

BEING PATIENT

Of course, I must issue a word of caution here. You might have had many, many lifetimes of projecting negative emotions into the physical. This is not something that can be undone overnight even though it can be undone in a relatively short period of time, relatively short compared to the time spent to create this negative momentum. But nevertheless, one of the strengths of the emotions is that they are less fleeting than thoughts, which means that they can give you a more long-term determination to keep carrying on.

You will see, for example, that when people have a positive goal and a positive feeling about reaching that goal, then those feelings will keep them going for a very long time in pursuit of the goal. This is the feeling that we hope to invoke in you so that you will not simply give these invocations for a couple of days and then be discouraged when no miraculous result is forthcoming.

You will have and gradually expand and build that positive feeling that will keep you going. You will keep using our tools, keep looking for new Aha experiences by studying our teachings, by practicing the invocations. And you will simply keep going with this even beyond a certain physical result because you realize that even though it may take a long time to attain a certain physical result, it does not take a long time to achieve results that you notice at the emotional, mental, and identity levels. Because you will begin to feel better about life, about yourself. You will begin to think more positively, and you will begin to realize and accept that you are a spiritual being, you are here for a purpose, a positive purpose.

Ah, my beloved, if you will but give these invocations a chance – if you will but give us a chance to guide you – you will begin to experience healing at all levels of your life. Be not so fixated on a particular physical result that you overlook the other results, for truly there may be things that are difficult to heal at the physical level, or that at least may take some time, for the cause is buried very deeply in the three higher levels.

DISEASES THAT CANNOT BE HEALED

There may be reasons why you carry a certain disease: to help others learn a lesson, or to carry and hold a certain spiritual balance for the collective consciousness. Thus, there are certain diseases or handicaps that you have to learn to live with. But part of your divine plan in these cases is to learn to live with it in the most positive way so that even if you have a disease or handicap, you can fulfill your divine plan, you can still be a positive person who uplifts all of those around him or her.

What I am saying is that you can gradually come to know this and that we will help you know this, whether a certain condition is part of your divine plan. Then, we will help you learn to deal with that condition in the highest possible way. Sometimes this, making peace with a condition, can bring healing. But if you have truly made peace with the condition, then it really is no longer an issue whether you have healing or not for you are living your life the way you are meant to live it, according to your own divine plan, the plan that you chose to formulate along with your divine teachers before you came into this lifetime, which is just one among many lifetimes. Therefore, when you begin to see this, you gain the cosmic perspective that perhaps it is not really so important what happens to you personally, for it is more important that you fulfill the long-term goal for this short-term engagement in the Globe Theater on earth.

MIRACLES

Kuan Yin I AM. I AM the Goddess of Mercy. I have often been prayed to by people expecting miracles. But the miracle is always a shift in consciousness. And only if that shift occurs, will there be a physical miracle. And then really, when the shift has occurred, where is the miracle except if you see life itself as one ongoing miracle of such incredible beauty of unfolding this almost unfathomable complexity that you see in the universe of your physical body, its cells and atoms and systems. Or you see it in the cosmos, in the cosmic dance of the galaxies and solar systems. What beauty all around you. What beauty all within you. For even though the current human body may not be the highest possible design, there is still incredible beauty to be found in your cells, in your atoms, in your organs, in how everything is orchestrated in this cosmic dance.

I know that when you have a physical disease, you might be focused on what does not work. But allow yourself to once in a while consider the miracle that so many trillions of cells can be organized in one coherent unit and can actually function to allow you to move around in the body and do things in the physical world. Is it not a miracle when you look at this? Is it not a miracle to realize that when you do not interfere with the function of the body, with a limited identity, limited thoughts and non-constructive emotions, then the four spirits – the elementary spirits that guide the unfoldment of your bodies – can and will manifest the perfect blueprint, even in the physical.

Ponder this. Ponder the other teachings that we have given and will give. But first of all, give the invocations. And always in the back of your mind ponder your attunement to the flow of the River of Life, for this attunement is the key to all healing. No matter what anyone might say, not matter what system or miracle cure they may come up with, there is really only one miracle cure and it is to flow with the River of Life. Flow, flow, flow, flow. This is the key that we give you in this matrix, this healing matrix that we have called the Song of Life.

So sing with us and let your energies flow. Let your thoughts flow. Let your identity flow towards higher and higher expression until you become that open door for the I AM Presence to express the perfect blueprint for this lifetime through you.

Kuan Yin I AM, and with my gratitude I give you my peace.

NOTE: The invocation corresponding to this chapter is:
Song of Life 3 – A New Emotional Body

Chapter 4

HEALING AT THE PHYSICAL LEVEL

My beloved heart, I AM Mary the Mother. I hold the office of the Divine Mother for planet earth. I hold each one of you in my heart. For there is none who can embody on planet earth without going through the Office of the Divine Mother and without having me, who is the head of that office, hold the spiritual balance for you at some level. Thus I can truly say that I have a personal, individual love for each of the almost 7 billion people in embodiment on earth, and even for those who are tied to earth while not presently being in a physical body.

YOU ARE A LIFESTREAM

As we have attempted to explain to you both in this teaching on the Song of Life but also in the many other teachings we have given, life does indeed have a purpose. You are not the product of a game of chance. Neither are you the product of an angry, judgmental God that will send you to hell if you do not function like a robot and blindly obey some dogma or some church leadership here on earth. You are a God-free co-creator, created to express your co-creative abilities in ways that would surprise even your Creator by the beauty and creativity that you can bring forth through your individual lifestream.

I know that traditionally many people who are open to the spiritual side of life believe that they are a soul that has embodied on earth. But many people also believe that the soul is something static, something that was created by God and therefore originally must have been perfect. And now it has embodied on earth and its role is to get back to that perfect state. But this is not a correct image.

The reality is that you were created as a lifestream, which means that you were created with a point-like sense of self, like the singularity that scientists say was the starting point of the physical universe. And you were meant to grow in self-awareness from that point-like sense of self to the all-encompassing sense of self of the Creator.

Thus, you are a life-stream, streaming from the singularity to the All-awareness that is your highest potential. You are not created in a static state of perfection even though there is a core of you that is pure awareness, but you are still created to expand your sense of self until you attain the awareness of being a Creator who can create its own universe, its own world of form.

Why am I telling you that you are a lifestream? Why are we telling you that you are meant to flow with the River of Life? Because what is disease? It is when something has blocked the flow. At the surface level something has blocked the flow of spiritual energy through the four lower bodies that you use here on earth. But on a greater level something has blocked you from seeing yourself as a lifestream.

You might think that you have come out of a static state. You might think that you are supposed to work towards a static state where you are supposedly saved and now sit on a pink cloud in heaven playing a harp for all eternity. Is that really a vision that you would like to attain—that state of being static for all eternity? I think not, for I know that you are created to be a lifestream, constantly flowing, constantly growing, constantly expanding, constantly becoming more, constantly co-creating that which is more.

THERE IS NO PERFECT HEALTH

Thus, what is the entire point of this healing matrix of the Song of Life? It is to get you back to the point where you see yourself as the flowing stream, and where you see that the stream of God's energy, the stream of the Holy Spirit, the stream of the River of Life is flowing through the four lower vessels that you use here in this physical universe on planet earth. Be that stream, and stream on and let God stream on through you.

What, then, is disease in the physical body? It is a message that at some level you are not streaming, you are not flowing with the River of Life. Thus, indeed, the only way to true healing, lasting healing, is to get back to the flow.

Look at how you have been brought up to look at the physical body, where you think there is supposed to be some normal state of health, which is what many of you at least have endured in much of your lifetime. You think that if your body now begins to show symptoms of disease, something has gone wrong and then you are supposed to get back to this state, this static state of good health.

But I tell you there is no static state of good health, even though you may for a time have experienced having a physical body that you did not need to worry about because it just performed its functions so you could go on living the way you thought you were supposed to live, depending on how you were brought up to think you were supposed to live by a society that, as we have said, wishes to control you in many ways.

What I am saying here is this: We have attempted to explain this from several angles and Master MORE has given a magnificent explanation of this at the end of his book [The Creative Power Within]. What I am saying is this: You cannot recreate perfect health for you cannot recreate what you never had. You have never had perfect health in your physical body. You may have had a state where you thought that you did not have to worry about your body, but that was not perfect health.

There is nothing static in the physical universe. Everything is constantly flowing and changing. It is only the ego, the outer mind, that creates the image that things stand still, that you can own something, that you can maintain and keep it over time. For I tell you there is nothing static in the physical universe. As we have said, everything is a projection, projected many times every second. And the screen upon which it is projected is constantly moving. As you know from physics and astronomy, the entire universe is expanding.

NOTHING IN THIS WORLD STANDS STILL

How do you think the universe can be expanding? You may have been taught that all of the galaxies, the millions and billions of galaxies, are constantly moving away from each other. But I tell you that there are some physicists who are closer to the truth – although not quite at the truth – when they say that it is as if all of the galaxies where drawn onto the surface of a balloon and the balloon is being blown up. And as the balloon expands, it seems as if the galaxies are moving further and further away from each other.

The reality here is that the entire world of form is a flowing stream of consciousness. We have said that you are just living in that stream, that the earth is just one speck of dust in the physical universe but that the physical universe is not an isolated universe. The Holy Spirit, the River of Life, is a constantly flowing stream. Space itself is constantly being stretched and expanded and you are being expanded with it. This is what drives the earth to rotate around the sun, or drives the sun to rotate around its galactic center, or drives the entire galaxy to rotate around its center and all of the galaxies to move in a coordinated symphony of life.

Your ego, the false teachers of the fallen ones, even your physical senses to some degree, want you to think that there is something in this giant stream to which you can hold on. But there is nothing that stands still. But what you can hold on to as the stable center of life is pure awareness, pure awareness that helps you see that even though you are in this physical octave, where everything is constantly changing, you do not have to be constantly changing with the circumstances you see around you. Instead you are the open door for your I AM Presence.

Your I AM Presence is not static. Your I AM Presence is flowing with the stream of life, and thus it is constantly transcending itself. Thus, you need only change along with the Presence as it transcends itself. You actually do not need to change with the changing circumstances on earth except where those changes are in line with the stream of the River of Life.

THE TWO TYPES OF CHANGES

Do I sound cryptic? I am indeed meaning to give you a bit of a riddle, for you realize that there are two kinds of changes. I know you have been brought up to be unaware of this. But there is the change that is self-transcendence that is constantly transcending itself and this is the River of Life. In the original design of the Elohim, the earth would start out at a certain level and then it would constantly transcend that level as those who embodied here co-created higher abundance in nature and in their own lives and society. This is the flow of the River of Life. And certainly, you want to flow with that.

But on earth you do not have the ideal situation, as we have said many times. Humankind has separated itself from the River of Life, and thus it has created its own spiral. It is not an upward spiral that leads to transcendence. It is a downward spiral that leads you to narrow your opportunities so that things begin to break down instead of self-transcend. These are the changes you see many times in society, even to some degree in nature.

My beloved, you do not need to adapt to these changes. Seeking to adapt to such changes is what causes you to block your creativity because you become trapped in what is the essential lie of what Jesus called the prince of this world. The lie is this: Spirit must adapt to the current conditions in matter.

This is what Peter said to Jesus when Jesus told his disciples what should happen to him. Peter refused to accept this because he thought it was beneath Jesus. And Jesus turned to Peter and said with a stern rebuke—I can assure you, for Jesus could be extremely stern: "Get thee behind me Satan." You may find occasion to use that statement yourself when you realize that you are being subjected to a projection from the collective consciousness, from the prince of this world that says: "You must adapt to the current imperfect situation on earth."

DO NOT ACCEPT ANYTHING FINAL

You have no obligation to adapt to the current imperfect situations on earth. Doing so will only cause disease in your body.

Therefore, likewise, if a doctor says to you: "You have a terminal illness" or: "You have an illness that cannot be healed," you have no obligation to accept this. I am not in any way saying that you should refuse medical treatment, for this is not what we teach. We teach that you must make use of whatever is available to you in society, both in the formal healing apparatus and in the more holistic and natural healing. We are not saying that you should refuse any form of healing that is available to you. On the contrary, pursue all of them as you are guided through your intuition. But nevertheless, do not accept the image that your physical body has now passed some kind of threshold and it can never again be well.

Yet, on the other hand, reach back to what I said earlier. You cannot re-create perfect health for imperfect health is a sign that you have separated yourself from the River of Life. Therefore, the way to heal is to get back into the flow so that instead of trying to re-create a previous state, you are not trying to turn back the clock, not even the body clock. You are flowing into a new and higher state than you could ever envision before.

A DEFINITION OF DISEASE

Thus, what is disease? We have told you that you have an individual divine plan that you yourself made along with your spiritual counselors before you took embodiment. There are some cases, as Kuan Yin explained, where an illness and dealing with an illness or healing an illness is part of your divine plan. There are also times – and this is most often the case – where an illness is not part of your divine plan. Therefore, you can look at an illness as a sign that you are not following your divine plan. But even if an illness is part of your divine plan, then the illness is still a sign and thus the universal teaching I want to give you is that any physical illness is a sign that you must change something.

If the illness is not part of your divine plan, then you should see the illness as a sign that you are not flowing with your divine plan, you are not in tune with your divine plan. And why not? Because throughout your upbringing you have come to accept these false images that are circulating in the collective consciousness on earth. You have come to think that your life should be a certain way, that you should live a certain way, that life should unfold a certain way.

One aspect of this among many is the idea that you should have the health that allows you to fulfill a certain job. And then you go through whatever process you go through until you get that job. And then you keep working at that job for 30, 40, or 45 years until you retire. And your body is simply supposed to adapt and function no matter how much stress you expose it to as a result of the job you are having.

But you see, in this day and age there are millions of spiritual people who have taken embodiment precisely in order to help bring about a new and better age based on a more spiritual approach to life. It is not in your divine plan to work like a robot for 40 or 45 years to make money for a privileged elite who do not share it with the people.

Thus, is it any wonder that when you go too far beyond what is in your divine plan, your body begins to show you a sign that something must change? Then, of course, if you truly want healing, you must use the tools we have given you – our teachings and these healing matrices – to bring yourself back where you have a clear vision of your divine plan. And for many people that means they have to be willing to rethink their life, to reconsider their life and their approach to life. Is it really right for you to work in a certain stressful job for 40 years or more? Is that really what you want to do in life? Then why have you allowed yourself to come to think that this is what you have to do, that you are stuck in this job, that there is no alternative?

THERE IS ALWAYS AN ALTERNATIVE

My beloved, one of the basic messages of any true spiritual teaching is this: There is always an alternative. There is always a different way to look at life. There is always a different way to react to life. When you pursue that different approach, visions will open up that you could not even dream about before because you would have immediately rejected them as unrealistic before you allowed yourself to consider that they might become reality.

This, then, is the message of the current medical profession and the health establishment on earth: You are supposed to live a productive life. If something goes wrong with the health of the body, the medical establishment will step in and try to fix the symptoms so you can go back to living a so-called productive form of life. But in some cases it does not work. For unknown reasons the disease will not go away, and then you just have to accept that you have to live with that disease and take medicaments for the rest of your life—or you will die from that disease.

When you become ill, and preferably before you become ill, is it not an opportunity, my beloved, to rethink that approach to life, that mechanical approach? Does there not come a time in your life, whether ill or not, where it is time to step back and rethink? For certainly, if your body is ill and you have had to take time off from your stressful lifestyle to focus on healing the body, do you not have the space and the time and the space in your mind to step back and rethink: "What is my divine plan? What is my highest potential for this embodiment? What can I learn? What can I express? Which gift can I give to the people around me or the planet at large? What can God bring forth through me in the remainder of this lifetime?"

Instead of thinking: "Oh but I do not have perfect health, how can I be of service to life," you focus on giving that service. And then you accept that you will have the health necessary for your service to be fulfilled. You accept this as a reality for you are now attuned to the flowing stream of your divine plan. You know you live not to have a comfortable lifetime, not to be a productive consumer. You live to fulfill your divine plan.

You accept and demand and you call into manifestation the health, the wealth and the outer circumstances that you need in order to fulfill your divine plan. Be not hung up on the specific vision of certain outer circumstances that you must have. Be flexible. Reach up for a higher vision and be willing to begin expressing your higher potential, your divine plan, with what you have right now, even if it is a physical illness.

Do something you have not done before. Reach out to help others in some way. Perhaps join the process of helping other people escape the same disease. Help create awareness about the disease. Help create awareness about the cause of disease, even beyond the physical to the emotional, mental and identity level causes of disease.

Seek to increase awareness of the spiritual side to life. Seek to teach others how it has comforted you in your illness and how it may comfort others. My beloved, I do not wish to here give you a matrix for what you personally should do, I am only suggesting that there are many options for what you could do no matter what your situation might be. There is always something you can do to reach beyond yourself. Do you not see that many people, as they become elderly and ill, they become more and more focused on themselves until their entire focus on life is so narrow that they are almost unreachable? And then what is the purpose of you being in embodiment if there is no focus beyond yourself? How can you flow with your divine plan if you only focus on the narrow self? Your divine plans seeks to raise all life including yourself, but not exclusive to yourself.

THE KEY IS TO FLOW

This, then, is the key, my beloved: Flow with life. Flow from where you are now into better health. Then flow into better health. Then flow into better health. Flow into a better reaction. Flow into an even better reaction. Flow into a more love-based rather than fear-based reaction. Flow into gratitude. Flow into gratitude for the opportunity to be alive, to have self-awareness, to have a physical body through which you can express something. Flow, my beloved. Change the way you look at life. Change the way you look at reality.

Use the invocation for the Song of Life. Use the physical aspect of that invocation, that I introduce, to call into manifestation in the physical the perfect health of your body, its organs and systems and cells and atoms. Call it into manifestation. Demand that it be manifest. See it as manifest. Accept it as manifest. Accept that it can be manifest. Accept that it is manifest.

As Jesus said: "Believest thou that I have the power to do this?" Believest thou that the Christ in you, that God in you, that the I AM Presence has the power to manifest the health you need to fulfill your divine plan? If you do not believe this, change your perspective. Work on changing your emotional, mental and identity bodies. For when you clear your mental body of the fear and doubt, when you clear your emotional body of the confusion and doubt, when you clear your identity of the belief that you are a human being limited by physical circumstances, well then you will know the reality that we have taught you: that this physical world, including the physical body, is but a mirage. That solidity is all camouflage. That there is nothing permanent here and that your physical body is being recreated many times every second. And why should it not be possible to recreate it in perfect health or in a more youthful appearance and function?

It is possible. It is possible. But it can only happen through the four levels of your mind. And thus, if you believe that it is not possible, then you will block the manifestation of it.

You have free will of what you allow to remain in your four lower bodies. And what you allow to remain there will block the manifestation of what is in your divine plan for your health, your wealth, your outer situation. Only you can block it with your beliefs that you dare not question, with your doubts, with your fears, with your anger and your negative feelings, with your lack of gratitude, with your lack of optimism and willingness to flow with life, to change as life needs to change as your I AM Presence wants to express a higher manifestation. Only you can block it.

DECIDE THAT YOU ARE WILLING TO CHANGE

I am not saying this to make you feel bad and give you an extra burden of guilt. I am saying this to galvanize you to make the decision that you are willing to change, to change your attitude and change your outlook. For this I trust you see can be changed regardless of what happens at the physical level. You can change something. You can always change something.

So, decide: "I am willing to change." And ask me or any other representative of the Divine Mother: "Help me change. Help me see how I can change." I have given a concept that while Jesus was young and growing I held the immaculate concept for him and for what was his Christ potential, the potential of his mission. I did not know in all details what it was but I knew some of what it was, and I held the vision for him. I hold the vision for each one of you. I will teach you to hold the immaculate concept for yourself if you will ask me, and if you will be willing to surrender, to give up, to let go of the false visions that you have come to accept as a result of growing up in this present lifetime, and that you have accepted in many previous lifetimes.

I am on the fifth ray of vision. I will give you a higher vision as you are willing to look beyond your present limited vision. Without vision the people perish. Without vision bodies perish. Without vision feelings perish. Without vision thoughts perish. Without vision identities, selves, perish. For without vision you cannot transcend the self, and that which cannot be transcended will be broken down by what we have called the second law of thermodynamics or the wrath of Kali or the force of Shiva or the spiritual fire that burns all that which stands still, which does not transcend.

Look into an open fire if you have a fireplace. See how the wood is transformed, how that physical form that seems fairly solid is transformed into a higher energy state where the atoms vibrate at a higher rate. Thus, the molecular bonds are broken down and the atoms are set free. A disease in your body is a solidified state where the atoms of your body are trapped in a certain matrix. By invoking the spiritual fire through our invocations and by shifting the awareness that holds them in that matrix, you can free the atoms. You can free the cells. Thus, your body can be recreated almost instantly in a higher matrix according to that immaculate vision, that immaculate concept that I hold in my mind, that your I AM Presence holds for you. And it is just a matter of what you can accept, what you can hold in the four levels of your mind. Only that determines what will be manifest in the physical.

ASK FOR MOTHER MARY'S HELP

Thus, my message is this: Study our teachings. Give our invocations. Call to us to help you shift your awareness. But first of all just this one simple thing: Be willing to change something.

There are those who say when you have fallen ill: "What do you have to lose? How could it get worse?" If you are already dying, why not try something radically different that you have never tried before. And even if you are not dying and hopefully long before you even manifest an illness, I am hoping you can see the need to try something that you have never done before: to shift your awareness, to shift your approach.

Thus, indeed, I can assure you that there were many times as Jesus was growing up where I had to direct him away from a self-destructive track and direct him back towards a positive track. I had to be quite stern with him sometimes to get him to the point where he himself had a vision that he had a mission in life and now he could begin to direct himself. I am willing to do the same for you, my beloved, if you will but ask, if you will but listen for the answers from within as you continue to give our invocations and study our teachings. I will surely find ways to whisper in your ear what you need to hear if you are willing to hear it without fear.

My beloved, there is nothing in the physical octave that cannot be changed. There is nothing that cannot be changed. Did you hear me? There is no thing that cannot be changed for no thing exists in and of itself. Every thing is a projection of a matrix, a mental matrix. Change the matrix and you change the thing. This is the law of God.

You were not brought up with an understanding of this law, but why should that prevent you from accepting its reality when it is presented to you? Be willing to make that shift. Give our invocations. Study our teachings. And you will be surprised how, before too long, you will look back at life and be amazed at how much you have shifted in such a short period of time. You may be amazed at how much your outer situation, including your physical health and the state of your wealth, has shifted in such a short period of time.

Prove me herewith and I shall pour you out a blessing – we who are representatives of the Divine Mother shall pour you out a blessing – so that there shall not be room in your mind to receive it. But as you expand your mind there will be room to receive it and thus it will be physically manifest.

For this I AM: the Master of Precipitation. And I am here to help you be a master of precipitation without trepidation. And thus, I bid you a fond adieu, but hoping that I can work with you on a continuous basis to help you shift your sense of self to the highest possible potential already written into your divine plan.

Mary the Mother I AM. I am the mother of the Christ child in you. Forget me not.

NOTE: The invocation corresponding to this chapter is:
Song of Life 4 – A New Body

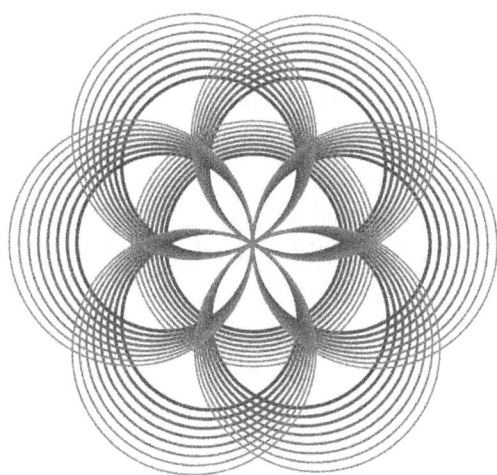

Chapter 5

Balance is the key to manifestation

Portia, I AM. I hold a spiritual office normally called the Goddess of Justice. Yet I am also the Goddess of Opportunity, for what is justice if not opportunity? You may not see it this way based on your upbringing on earth, where you have often seen the pictures of the Goddess of Justice as a female figure holding up the scales in one hand, perhaps even a sword in the other hand, and then being blindfolded.

But why is the Goddess of Justice blindfolded? And why are the scales out of balance? Well, because humankind is out of balance. Human beings are out of balance in their individual consciousness, and the collective consciousness is out of balance. When you are out of balance, you do not see with clear vision. Instead, you see with polluted perception, and you project your perception upon everything around you.

THE GODDESS OF JUSTICE IS NOT BLIND

That is why human beings have projected their unbalanced perception upon the Goddess of Justice, thinking that she must be blind for allowing the many things that happen on earth, that they see happening around them. For if the Goddess of Justice was not blind, how could this or that or the next thing be allowed to happen?

But you see, the Goddess of Justice, the office that I hold, has little to do with the standards of justice that human beings have created on earth. When you are in the consciousness of separation you will, as we have explained many times, see yourself as being in opposition to others. If those others do not submit to the way you think things ought to be, then you develop a desire to fight them or to destroy them or to punish them. If you do not have the power to do this yourself, then you will want God to do this for you.

Why do you not have the power to do this yourself? Because, as we have explained, once you go into separation you inevitably become trapped in the pattern of action and reaction. When you react to circumstances in an unbalanced way, your reaction becomes an unbalanced action that you project into the cosmic mirror. What can the mirror reflect back to you except similarly unbalanced physical circumstances?

You may think that other people are doing something to you that is unjust. But according to the Law of God, they would not be able to do that to you if you were in complete harmony and balance—with the exception of those who are so balanced that they serve as the judgment for those who will violate even the innocent. Yet this is also within the greater framework of the Law of Free Will.

Thus, it truly can be said that there is no injustice in the universe. Because on a planet like earth, where you know you are far below the ideal scenario – which all have known before they embodied here – then how can you really set up a standard that says that life on this planet should live up to a certain standard for justice? This planet is a laboratory that allows humankind to outplay their current state of consciousness and become each others karmic return, so to speak, from the cosmic mirror.

Human beings on earth often serve to mirror back to each other what they themselves have been projecting into the cosmic mirror. How, my beloved, can that be a lack of justice when you recognize the reality that the mirror cannot reflect back to you something that you have not sent out? Perhaps you sent it out in a past lifetime. Perhaps you cannot remember sending it out. But you did or it would not be reflected back to you.

WHY YOU HAVE BEEN VIOLATED

Now, in saying this we must, of course, allow for the outplaying of free will. Yes, it is possible that someone can do something to you because they are making a choice in the present. They are violating, for example, an innocent child who not even in past lives has made the choice that has created an action that is now being reflected back. In other words, the choice was not made by the child. That means the action is not a return from the cosmic mirror.

The situation, where for example, the child is violated was caused by the choices made by the adult in the present. Yet even this is a result of choices you have made when you volunteered to come into embodiment on a planet like earth, where you fully knew before you came here what you were getting into. You knew that part of your reason for coming was to be a Holy Innocent in embodiment. This means that there will be those who are trapped in the fallen consciousness who will attempt to violate you in some way or another. Do you understand what I am saying? You cannot embody on a planet like earth without being violated by those trapped in the fallen consciousness. It is simply impossible. This is something you will know before you voluntarily embody here.

I fully acknowledge that there are those who have not voluntarily embodied here because they have come from other planetary systems or they have fallen from higher spheres. But falling here or being assigned here was also a result of choices you made, and thus again your choices are responsible for you being here. If you volunteered to come here you made a choice to come here. You knew you would be violated by those in the fallen consciousness because they will be disturbed and provoked by the light that you bring.

MAINTAINING INNOCENCE

You knew that your challenge was to face this violation in whatever form it might take and then remain in innocence or get back to innocence as quickly as possible. What is innocence, my beloved? It is that you have no human, man-made expectations about what life should be on earth. You are like water. You flow. If you happen to flow over the edge of a cliff, then you fall down. But then you gather yourself and flow along. If you happen to be in a stale pond for a while, then when you become aware of this you rise above the edge and flow on. This is innocence.

For you are always flowing with the River of Life, flowing with the Holy Spirit, always willing to go where you are prompted to go in order to be of greater service to life. When you have fulfilled your reason for being in a certain place, you are open to flowing on, whatever the outer cost might be, for you seek here no continuing city. You seek to be an instrument while you are in embodiment. And then you seek to ascend and move on when it is time for you to do so. For how can you ascend and move on when you are holding on to anything on earth, such as a sense of injustice, a sense that there is something you must fix, something you must correct on earth?

It is very important for spiritual people to acknowledge the existence of fallen beings, of the fallen mindset and the duality consciousness. It is the only way you can truly move on from being stuck in the no-man's land, in the catch-22, in the enigma where the fallen ones attempt to put you so that you cannot manifest your Christhood and win your ascension, nor fulfill your divine plan while in embodiment. They seek to paralyze you so that you might carve out a comfortable life for yourself on earth. Or you may be uncomfortable, but either way you are not rising above a certain level of consciousness and therefore you do not manifest the Christhood that becomes a threat to their control of this planet.

One of the many schemes – one of the many, many schemes – created by them is precisely this subtle sense that we have called the epic mindset where you think that something has gone wrong with God's plan or God's law. That is why the scales held by the Goddess of Justice are out of balance. That is why she is blindfolded. And that is why someone should have a sword to punish those who are the guilty ones, for in the epic mindset there is always a scapegoat. Those other people are representing evil. They are the problem. They should be put down. They should be exterminated, or whatever you can come up with.

DIVINE JUSTICE

As long as you have this sense of injustice, you will be tied to earth karmically, for you are sending into the cosmic mirror the sense that something is wrong here, and that you are the one who can judge what is wrong and who is wrong and what should be done about it. For you do not trust that God can work this out by himself. You do not trust that divine justice actually works, and works with absolute accuracy.

You see, divine justice is that whatever you send out is mirrored back to you; or if you are one of the Holy Innocent that whatever happens to you on earth becomes the judgment of those in the fallen mindset and therefore helps to advance the growth of planet earth by them being judged and removed from this planet. But again, it was your choice to play this part by embodying on earth, and it is your responsibility to maintain your innocence or get back to it, for only then, when you have that innocence, will you be able to effortlessly flow when the Holy Spirit calls you to move on.

Only when you follow the one Holy Spirit will you be able to let go of the spirits you have created on earth, the spirits that keep you bound in a certain place, a certain mindset and level of consciousness. If you cannot flow then you must resist, for flow is the natural state of life. When you are in the state of innocence, you are flowing. For what is there to hold on to in innocence? What is there to correct? What image of earth is there to hold on to when you know that in this physical realm everything is in flux, everything is in movement and ultimately the appearances on this earth are not real. They have no power over you as a spiritual being. This is part of being an Innocent. You know that whatever thing may happen on earth cannot touch you as the pure awareness of the living Spirit.

I fully realize, for I am not blind to what is happening on earth, that there are many things on earth that are absolutely atrocious. But can you not step back for a moment and see that the fallen beings have created such circumstances precisely because the only way they can trap people in the action-reaction game is by violating people through an action that is so outrageous, so seemingly unjust, that people feel they have to act, they have to do something about it. Thus, they get trapped in reacting to the actions of the fallen beings. Or they even get trapped in seeking to punish the fallen beings or correct their injustices, whereby they send out their own action which is unbalanced and therefore must come back as an unbalanced reaction from the cosmic mirror.

Cosmic justice is that when you send out an action from a certain level of consciousness, that action will be sent back to you and it will take the form of unbalanced circumstances on earth. An unbalanced mind will lead to an unbalanced physical situation. Yet, when you strive for balance in your four lower bodies, as we have given you the tools to attain with the four previous teachings and invocations, then you can break this action and reaction game.

THE OPPORTUNITY TO BALANCE KARMA

I know well that many spiritual people are familiar with the concept of karma, that this is sort of a return of the actions you have taken in a past life. And many have come to have a certain fatalistic view that whatever impulse you have created in a past life must inevitably come back to you either in this life or in a future life. But this is not so. The cosmic law states that whatever you send out must come back to you as long as you remain in the same unbalanced state of consciousness from which you sent out the action.

But if you transcend that state of consciousness, then cosmic justice mandates that what you send out either will not come back to you as a physical circumstance, or you will have the tools and the knowledge of how to transmute the karma before it manifests in the physical. This is why my beloved consort, Saint Germain, asked for a dispensation back in the 1930s to publicly release knowledge of the violet flame and how to use it. This is why we have given you teachings on all of the seven rays now. For truly, while the violet flame is very efficient for consuming karma, you really need to invoke the light of all seven rays in order to consume the karma you made through unbalanced use of any one of the seven rays.

You see, while the violet flame can indeed prevent ancient karma from coming back in the physical, it cannot transcend the karma at the emotional, mental and identity levels. For in order to do that, you must invoke the light of the particular ray that you misqualified in creating that karma.

What I seek to convey here is this: When you have used our tools to purify your four lower bodies, there may come a point where you feel like even though you have done all these things spiritually – perhaps doing many other things than what we are giving you here – you are still not getting the results you are hoping for. You are not having the manifestation you are wanting to see, whether it be health or wealth, whether it be a different situation, whether it be a different relationship, whether it be an opportunity to serve in a better way. You feel you are treading water. But you see, what you need to consider then is the need to look at your own consciousness and discover any elements of imbalance.

LOOK FOR IMBALANCED BELIEFS

It is possible to purify your four lower bodies but still maintain certain imbalanced viewpoints, certain imbalanced beliefs about life, including, as I described, the belief that something has gone wrong on earth, that there is an injustice, that it needs to be corrected and that someone needs to do so including yourself. But you see, when you act from this imbalanced mindset, you cannot escape the action-reaction sequence.

You are trapped in this closed loop where, as we have said, you are actually reacting to the unbalanced actions that you yourself sent out in the past. But you are still projecting that it is other people who are responsible for your reactions, or it is God or fate that is responsible for your reactions. The only thing left is for you to look at this, for you to take responsibility for your reactions and say: "Why do I react this way?"

You may, if you are willing to do so, actually use an ability we have described before where if you center in your heart and tune in to your heart chakra in the center of your chest, you have there a very fine measuring instrument that actually can help you evaluate everything you encounter on earth. Master MORE has explained *[The Creative Power Within]* that whenever you encounter something – an idea or a situation – you can apply the measurement: "Is it raising or is it lowering my energies?"

But there is another way to use this intuitive ability, and that is to imagine that in the heart chakra you see the scales, just as you see being held up by the Goddess of Justice where you have the two bowls hanging from a rod that is balanced. And now you envision this – you tune in to this in your heart – and then you sense: Is one bowl lower than the other? If so, you know that something is weighing down that bowl. And then you look at the teachings we have given on the duality consciousness that there are always two polarities, and then you see that the reason for this is that you have an imbalance, but you have an imbalance in two places.

On the one side there is a viewpoint to which you are very attached, that you are very sure is right. And this creates such a focus of your mental energies that the mental energies have the mass to take that side of the scale down. But on the other side there is an opposite polarity where you also have an imbalanced view, where there is something you are not seeing, or something you think is unimportant or which you take too lightly. And therefore there is not enough mass on that side to weigh down that scale.

How do you balance the scales? Well, is the simplest way not to take something off one side and to add something to the other side until you have balance? For I am not here talking about the grey thinking of compromising, of thinking you just have to be nice, loving and kind to everyone. I am talking about true Christ discernment where you are willing to look at the imbalances on both sides and correct those imbalances by reaching for the Christ mind. This is truly what we have given you ample teachings and tools for attaining. You can examine your attitude and beliefs about life and readjust them based on that central rod that is holding up the scales. It is the rod of Christ that is anchored in the rock of Christ.

You see, this is oneness where it is standing vertically and nothing can topple it for it will not lean to either side. Thus, it is the fixed point. The scales, the bowls, are hanging from a horizontal rod that is balanced in its center exactly over this immovable rock of Christ. But how long is that horizontal bar holding up the two bowls?

A NEW SENSE OF SELF THROUGH BALANCE

My beloved, we have said that you start embodying for the first time on earth with a point-like sense of self. This might be compared to being so narrow that you really cannot go to either side and therefore, in a sense, you cannot become imbalanced. But on the other hand you have a very narrow sense of self-awareness. So how then do you expand your sense of self-awareness towards the 144th level? By expanding the horizontal rod of your personal scale of life.

The longer the horizontal rod is, the wider is your sense of self, the more encompassing is your sense of self and the closer you are to the 144th level. Yet, when you think about simple geometry, my beloved, the simple geometry of levers, you see that as the horizontal rod becomes longer and longer, each side forms a lever, which means that it now takes less and less weight to get the scale to be out of balance.

What does this mean? It means that when you are at lower levels of the path, such at the 48th level and the few above it, you can allow yourself to have somewhat extreme viewpoints. You are still young and you are experimenting and you need to try out different things to see what works and what does not work. There is nothing wrong with, as you see in children, that they might express very absolutist, very firm viewpoints about this and that aspect of life, but this is natural for children to do.

But you also see in many cases that as people grow up they somewhat moderate their views and become more aware that there could be different ways to look at things and that they might all be valid in certain circumstances. You have a more nuanced, more balanced, more encompassing view of life. And this is what I am seeking to teach you here.

The closer you move to the higher levels of consciousness, the more important it is to be in balance. Therefore, even a small imbalance in your viewpoints about life can have the effect of bringing one bowl down and raising one bowl up. And my beloved, that is why you feel like you are treading water and that things are not manifesting, because you are too imbalanced. I can assure you that until your scale is balanced, you will not have the manifestation that you seek.

WHAT STOPS MANIFESTATION

You see, you might think of it this way: As you purify your four lower bodies here in the material realm, you are working in the lower figure, the lower half, of a figure-eight. The nexus of the figure-eight is in the dividing line between the material world – the four levels of the material world – and the spiritual where your I AM Presence resides.

As you are purifying your four lower bodies, you are creating a momentum, a movement, that goes through the lower half of the figure-eight, starts to go up the figure-eight, and now it hits the nexus and it creates a momentum that goes up in the upper figure of the figure-eight. Once it is up here, it has achieved what scientists hope to achieve when they search for superconductivity where a current can move through a material without resistance. In other words, the impulse you send into the spiritual realm will be multiplied by your I AM Presence and it will then go back down the figure-eight until it reaches the nexus.

But the thing is, the closer you get to Christhood, the more important it is that you are balanced. Because when you attain Christhood, you – meaning the Conscious You, your sense of self, your sense of awareness – you are sitting right there in the nexus. For what is the nexus? It is a singularity. Where is the room for imbalance in a singularity?

Thus, you may have, in past lives and in this life, used spiritual tools and done good works to create the return current from the universe, from your I AM Presence. But as you get closer to Christhood, even the smallest imbalance can prevent the return current from going through the nexus and entering the physical realm.

I can tell you that there are many, many spiritual people who have, as we have said, laid up treasures in heaven. They have created what you might call positive karma both in this and in past lives. It is ready to break through to the physical and manifest. But why is it not breaking through? Because there is still some imbalance.

Actually, in your higher vision, in your higher will, you do not want the positive return to break through because then that imbalance would misqualify and misdirect the light. Thus, you yourself would rather have it held back than have it be misqualified. And that is what I am seeking to help you see here—that many sincere spiritual people have already created a return current that could break through and manifest in their lives as better circumstances: be it health, be it wealth, be it an opportunity to serve. But it is not breaking through because there is still some little imbalance.

For many of you it is a very small imbalance. And it is our hope that with all of the invocations and teachings we have released here, along with all of the invocations and teachings for the seven rays in the books that are and will be forthcoming, we can give you that impetus that can help you finally see what is out of balance, finally see it, finally let go of that spirit, let go of that decision, and then cosmic justice will manifest in your life.

My beloved, it is not I, Portia, nor is it the members of the Karmic Board who are holding back your just return for your efforts. It is you yourself because you do not want that return to become affected by that little imbalance you still hold in your being. Do you see? That is why we say there is no injustice in the universe.

SEEK HIGHER VISION

Get in touch with your own higher vision, your own higher being. See that one imbalance or those few imbalances still remaining. Let them go, my beloved. Let them go. Come to that perfect center where you are in the nexus of the vertical figure-eight flow, and you are in the center of the horizontal balancing rod of your consciousness, where your consciousness is the widest, the most encompassing, yet you are still in complete balance.

That is the point of stillness where you can know: "I am still and I am God. And therefore, I am as above and so below." And that is the manifestation you want. You do not want a manifestation that is unbalanced here below and not a reflection of what is above. You want to be as Above so below and that is why you, without being aware of it, are holding back the manifestation so that you will not have an unbalanced manifestation in your life that will create another action-reaction sequence that you need to balance and deal with.

You do not want to repeat these patterns, and that is why you yourself are holding it back, waiting for yourself to attain that perfect balance that then opens up the floodgates of heaven and brings into manifestation the return current of the promise made: "Prove me now herewith, saith the lord, that I shall pour you out a blessing that there shall not be room enough to receive it."

That blessing can come, but it will not come until you are willing to have it come because you know that you are in balance and can receive it in a balanced manner. Do you see my beloved? You are your own worst critic, but you are in a sense also your own best teacher, for you are the one deciding when and how you want things to manifest in your life.

The key is to become more aware of your subconscious attitudes and beliefs and how any imbalance will prevent the manifestation that you desire. You will of course also look at your desires and make sure that they are not imbalanced, and certainly not imbalanced by the epic mindset wanting to correct some injustice by punishing or destroying others or by having God punish or destroy them. If your God is an angry and vengeful God in the sky, then right there you have a major imbalance that will prevent the manifestation.

SEEKING BALANCE OPENS MANIFESTATION

Manifestation, my beloved. Ponder this for there is no force in heaven that will hold back your co-creative powers. You are the one who is holding it back either through an imbalance so that you cannot even send anything up to heaven that can be multiplied and sent back, or because you know you are not yet there where you can receive the return current and use it wisely.

Thus, again, I say to you: seek balance. For only in the balance can you flow with the River of Life. And as we have hopefully helped you see, the flow is life. You may think of the scales as being stationary, but they are not. For as we have explained to you, there is a current, an undercurrent called the River of Life, the Holy Spirit. And the key to flowing with that current is to have your personal scales in balance because when they are not in balance you are going to and fro and back and forth and using up a lot of energy resisting the flow of the River of Life, getting it to go where you think is should go instead of simply surrendering into it, flowing with it, and letting the Spirit take you where you can be of greatest service.

This is the key to flowing with the River of Life. It is selfless service where you let go of these expectations and desires that are centered around yourself as a being, but you realize you are part of the great mind of God, you are part of the all, and you are here only to help raise the all, not for self-centered purposes.

Thus, there are some of you who still have some self-centered desires and dreams about being famous and having recognition or having money or having power to correct this or that wrong or awaken other people or whatever it may be. And this is why you are subconsciously holding back the manifestation because your desires, your vision, is not balanced.

My beloved, I truly have only one desire for you, and that is to see you achieve that balance so that you can flow with the River of Life, where you can fully embrace the realization that there is no injustice in the universe and that you are not bound by any conditions in the matter realm.

This is matter realization. When you realize that: "I am not matter and I am not bound by matter." Then you have a new reality and then you are in balance. And then you can be as Above so below.

My beloved, I am Above. I do not have an anchor in the physical octave. That is why I cannot manifest divine justice here below. I cannot become as Above so below, for I have ascended. The beauty and the wonder of you having not ascended is that you can become as Above so below.

But you cannot become here below as you are Above as long as you have these unbalanced beliefs, desires and ideas about how the universe should be run. Thus, be willing to flow with the Spirit here below for I can assure you, my beloved, the I AM Presence does flow with the Spirit Above. It does not flow according to man-made ideas and expectations. It flows with the Holy Spirit. And that is the key to being as Above so below.

Thus, I seal you in the love of the Cosmic Mother of Justice for earth, for that mother I AM. Portia is my name. May you go in the peace of knowing there is no injustice in the universe.

NOTE: The invocation corresponding to this chapter is:
Song of Life 5 – Manifestation

The key to
flowing with the River
of Life is to have your
personal scales in balance
because when they are not in
balance you are going to and
fro and back and forth and
using up a lot of energy
resisting the flow of the
River of Life.

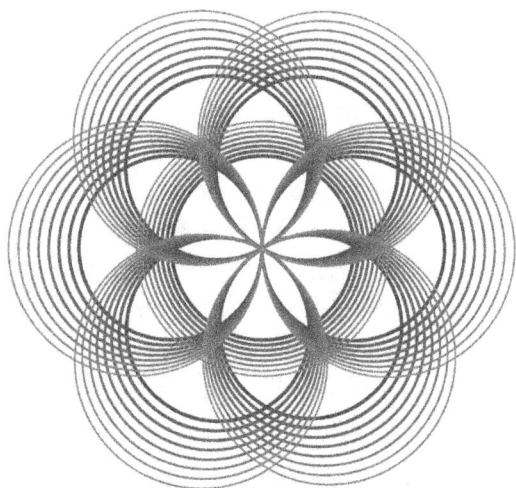

Chapter 6

UPHOLD YOUR TORCH
OF SPIRITUAL LIGHT

Mother Liberty, I AM. The Goddess of Liberty, I AM. I AM the representative of the Divine Mother who for earth holds the spiritual balance that seeks to set all people free from the limitations they face in the mother realm, the Ma-ter realm.

Yet I do not only seek to set you free from physical limitations. I seek to set you free from the greater limitation that Mother opposes your freedom, that matter restricts your Spirit. For how can you come to feel that matter restricts your Spirit? You can come to feel so only when you think there is a particular result you have to achieve so that matter somehow conforms to the vision you have of how matter should materialize.

THE TRUE MEANING OF LIBERTY

Do you see, my beloved, the subtle point I am seeking to expose here? Of course, if you already saw this, why would you need to study the teaching? But let me give you some hints that might trigger an inner knowing that you already have.

You have, of course, the physical focus of my flame, which is anchored over the Statue of Liberty in the New York harbor. You might know that during the decades when many, many people came to America from Europe and other parts of the world, they all had to enter through New York harbor. And one of the first things they would see would indeed be the Statue of Liberty standing there, welcoming them as the song goes: "Give me your tired and your poor, your huddled masses yearning to breathe free."

Indeed, most of the people who came after having made the sacrifice of giving up whatever they had or did not have – but nevertheless giving up that with which they were familiar in the so-called old world – they very much felt that they had very little opportunity, they had little justice, they had little freedom. And what they in most cases felt was that they did not have the opportunity to receive a just harvest of their hard work.

This is, of course, what had been taken away from people during those feudal societies in Europe where a small elite had set itself up so that the general population were literally the slaves of the elite, so that the general population had to work, but they could only reap the harvest that could barely keep them alive while the majority of the harvest was taken by the privileged elite.

This, of course, is still the way it is in many nations, including the United States which certainly does not live up to the ideals of equal opportunity or an equal reward for your effort, for there are still those who steal the efforts of the people. Nevertheless, that is a topic for another day.

What I wish to bring to your attention here is that the millions of people who came to the shores of the United States – and thus passed through the flame of the focus that I maintain over the Statue of Liberty – did indeed come hoping to receive greater liberty in the physical realm. They were often hoping to own their own piece of land, which was a seemingly impossible dream in Europe in those days. They were hoping that by working hard they would reap a just reward of their efforts and be able to build a good life for themselves and their families. But most of them were clearly focused on material needs, although some also came because they wanted the freedom from political oppression or from the oppression of the elite.

Nevertheless, very, very few of the people who came to these shores and saw the Statue of Liberty, becoming gradually more visible through the mist, understood the basic principle of liberty. Very few people understood what liberty really means.

SPIRITUAL LIBERTY

Surely, liberty has many aspects and one aspect is freedom from poverty because poverty is truly one of the worst forms of oppression in the material world. When you are poor and have to focus all of your energy and attention on barely existing, then how can you have much attention or energy left over to consider the deeper aspects of life or the purpose of life or spiritual growth? Thus, indeed, it is an unprecedented luxury and opportunity that so many people in the developed world today have free time and attention left over to consider the spiritual side of life.

It is truly one of the great opportunities for mankind that so many people have pursued spiritual growth and are pursuing spiritual growth through whatever means they see available to them. Every single person who sincerely strives to raise his or her consciousness is contributing to the building of a better age.

Nevertheless, of all the millions of people who pursue spiritual growth, very few have started to realize what it really means to win your spiritual liberty. What is it you are liberated from when you become truly free? Well, you are liberated from the state of consciousness that dominates this earth. We have called it the fallen consciousness, the duality consciousness, the consciousness of separation. But I will give you a little more information, a different perspective on it.

We have talked about those who come to this earth in Holy Innocence. They come with a desire to raise this planet up so that it becomes part of the ascending process, the Holy Spirit that raises this entire sphere of the material realm to the ascension point. They come with only one desire: To share their light, their spiritual light streaming from the I AM Presence.

Yet as we have attempted to explain, this planet is currently home to many lifestreams who are trapped in the fallen consciousness, the consciousness of duality and separation. This is, as Portia explained, part of cosmic justice, for these lifestreams have been given another opportunity. And there is no one who is forced to go to earth if they do not have past choices that actually magnetize them here or if they do not volunteer out of their innocence.

There is no one in heaven who is forced to come to earth. Those who descend in innocence volunteered, and those who come here because they have already embodied elsewhere come here as a result of choices they have made themselves. They do not always come here voluntarily in the sense that they can do anything they want. They come here because they are trapped by their own past choices and earth then becomes another opportunity, where they could not take advantage of the opportunity they had been given previously on another planet with a higher level of consciousness.

THE LIE THAT MOTHER IS LIMITED

So you see, cosmic justice is simple: The only thing that limits you is your own past choices. What could be more just than this? But then what is it that limits your past choices? Well, consider what happens when you come as one of the Innocent to this planet where so many are trapped in the fallen consciousness. They see you as a threat – they see your light as a threat – because it challenges their view of life. Their view of life is based on the duality consciousness. The consciousness of separation must, of necessity, create separation. This has many levels. People on earth see themselves as separated from their God, therefore they cannot accept what Jesus said: that the kingdom of God is within you.

But beyond that, people on earth see themselves as separated from each other. And when there is separation between different groups of people, there will be contradictions, disagreements, conflicts. And there will be a tendency that some will seek to dominate and control others. Those who are the most trapped in the duality consciousness will seek to set themselves up as a privileged elite. And in order to attain that state of privilege and maintain that state of privilege, they must keep the majority of the population in a state of being under control and of being in poverty or of not being in power. Yet in order to maintain this status quo, they must cause the majority of the population to shut off the flow of spiritual light through their beings.

They have created this consciousness that the Earth Mother, the Ma-ter realm, is inherently limited. There is only a limited amount of resources on earth and therefore only a small elite can be rich, whereas the majority of the population must be poor, or at least not as rich as the elite. You see this today in the United States where a great number of people have attained a certain status of middle class living that is good compared to that of previous generations, but you still have in the last several decades a smaller elite accumulating more and more wealth and more and more control over the financial and political systems of this nation. This is not justice. This is not the state that would exist if this planet was in balance. It is in a state of imbalance, and that is the only way that a small elite can gain privileges, wealth and control.

In order to maintain that status quo of being in a privileged position, they must cause the majority of the population to shut off the flow of spiritual light through their beings because that spiritual light acts exactly like the torch that the Statue of Liberty is holding up. It acts as a light in the darkness. And what does a light in the darkness do? It exposes the darkness.

When everything is dark, nobody really realizes it is dark. It is only when a beam of light starts shining that you suddenly look around and see how dark it was, for you were so used to it before that you did not even notice. You thought this was the way life had to be—this was the only way life could be in the material realm where everything is so limited. So how could it be otherwise than that there is only enough wealth for a small elite? This is the lie they have perpetrated for many centuries.

THE POWER TO DEFINE "REALITY"

How did they perpetrate this lie? How did they make the majority of people on this planet accept this lie? Well, they did so by creating what we have talked about before, the concept that there is a certain standard based on which everything should be evaluated, that there is a certain absolute truth and everything should be compared to that truth. But you see, if you create a mindset – which by the way the intellect, the analytical mind, loves – that there is one truth, one reality, to which everything else should be compared, then do you not see that whoever defines that one so-called reality has enormous power to control the minds of the people?

If you are the one setting the standard to which everyone else must compare, can you not see that this gives you enormous power? You become literally, as the serpent said to Eve in the Garden of Eden, as a god knowing good and evil for you are defining the standard that defines good and evil.

But beyond that, you define the mindset that everything should be compared to this standard. And this means that when a Holy Innocent comes to this earth and wants to express its light, it is suddenly now in an environment where it cannot just express its light. For when it does so, those who are in control, those who are the fallen beings – or even many among the general population who are the generally downtrodden – will immediately demand that the expression of your light should live up to the prevailing standard of the society in which you are expressing yourself.

SUBMISSION OR REBELLION

Once you take a standard based on separation and apply it to the expression of spiritual light, you will immediately – immediately, my beloved – create a tension in the being who is expressing the light. Now, you can avoid this tension by staying in innocence and continuing to express your light, but this is a very difficult initiation that most people who are new to this planet cannot pass right away. Most of the beings who have come here, including those of us who have ascended from this planet, have fallen prey to the fallen standard. We have therefore reacted to the standard. And there are two main reactions: You either submit or you rebel. You conform or you refuse to conform. Do you see the mindset that this now puts you in?

Holy Innocence means that you are a child at play. You are expressing your light creatively. Creativity has no standard. If you try to evaluate your creative expression based on a certain standard before you express yourself, you cannot be creative because now the standard will force you to either conform or rebel. And whether you conform or rebel, you are not creative in the higher understanding of that word.

What happened to the Innocents that came to this planet was that they were met with this intensely hostile, intensely aggressive, reaction from other people. There were those in control who did not want them to raise a torch that could expose their unbalance, their inequality, their darkness. They did everything in their power to squash you. But even many among the people did not want you to raise up a torch that could show them that one could be different on earth, that one did not have to submit to a standard.

They did not want to be disturbed in their victim consciousness, for they had come to see themselves as being inherently limited and therefore having to make the best of their lot by staying within boundaries. So you see, neither the leaders nor those who submitted to the leaders wanted anyone to rock the boat and demonstrate that one did not have to submit and one did not have to rebel by fighting the elite. There was a Middle Way, a different way, and it was to innocently and playfully express the light regardless of the reaction you got from other people. This is innocence. It is not innocence that you shut off your light.

What happened to those who could not remain the Innocent? As I said, most people, most beings, could not and it is perfectly understandable and natural. I am not in any way seeking to blame anyone for going into this pattern. I am simply seeking to help you understand what happened whereby you will also see how to extricate yourself from the pattern and attain liberty.

SHUTTING DOWN YOUR CREATIVITY

So what happened to the Innocents when they were met with this intensely hostile reaction? Well, what happened was natural. They said: "I do not want to deal with this hostility." But of course, they were in embodiment—they could not withdraw from being in embodiment. But what they really said was: "I do not want to be creative in an environment where my creativity is not appreciated but elicits such a hostile reaction." So in a sense you said: "I am alive. I will have to stay in embodiment. But I do not want to be here. I do not want to deal with this fallen consciousness. I do not want to deal with this hostility."

In order to maintain a life here and not have to deal with the hostility, you created the ego. You created an aspect of the ego to deal with this hostility and it can take various forms. One can be that you submit, you simply submit to the standard of society. You try to be a good citizen. The other can be that you become rebellious. You become like some of the artists you have seen who deliberately defy the norms of society. Or you try to create revolutions to overthrow the ruling elite whereby you inevitably become another elite. But you can also go into a reaction where you simply shut off creativity and try to live as best you can without living creatively, without challenging the status quo.

This aspect of the ego is precisely what takes away your liberty. For now you are constantly in this mindset of feeling that you have to adapt your life and your expression of who you are to this external standard. You are defining yourself in relation to this external standard on earth rather than defining yourself in relation to your I AM Presence in the spiritual realm.

That is why you cannot be an open door, because you are no longer a child at play who is willing to give expression to whatever impulse is sent from the I AM Presence. You have created a mind that sits between the I AM Presence and the expression of the Presence here below. This mind evaluates what is coming from the Presence, what is likely to be the reaction from the environment: "Do I want that reaction from the environment? No I do not, so then I will not allow the expression from the Presence to come forth."

This takes away not only your liberty but your joy and sense of purpose, your sense of playfulness. And now life becomes a grind, a treadmill. And that is why you become one of the tired, one of the poor, one of the huddled masses yearning to breathe freely, but thinking this means you must go somewhere else on earth and create different circumstances on earth. But you see, you may create different circumstances, you may have the outer impression that you are free, but no circumstance on earth can give you freedom because no circumstance on earth can take away your freedom. The only thing that can take away your liberty is that you use your own ability to shut off the creative flow from the Presence. That is what takes liberty.

MOTHER IS NOT YOUR ENEMY

Do you see, my beloved, the Mother is not your enemy? The Mother does not restrict you. It only mirrors back, as Portia said, what you are projecting out. And when you go into creating that ego to respond to the fallen beings and their consciousness, you are sending out that you want to be caught in this game.

Now, of course, you have deep within you the inner sense that in the spiritual realm, in reality, in the ideal scenario, you should have liberty to express your creativity. Therefore, there is a deep sense in you that if you are not allowed to express your creativity on earth, something must be wrong on earth. But you see, even this plays into the fallen beings who only want to keep you trapped in this pattern of either submitting to them or rebelling against them, but nevertheless always doing what you do in relation to them and their standard.

This is what takes away your liberty. It is not the Mother. It is not the mother realm. There are no inherent limitations in the mother realm that dictate that there is a lack of resources so that only a small elite can be rich. This earth could bring forth plenty of resources to feed 10 billion people who lived an affluent life where they never had to fear lack or poverty.

It is not just a matter of redistributing the resources that are already there—redistributing the wealth as the communists attempted to do. It is a matter of opening up the creative flow whereby Mother Earth suddenly will begin to outpicture what the abundance consciousness is projecting upon it.

You, of course, know deep within that things are not right on earth. But what I am trying to help you see here is that when you go into this mindset that you have to either submit or rebel against the fallen beings and their standard, you are not actually helping to improve things, you are simply maintain the status quo where the separate mindset, the dualistic mindset, is dominating earth and therefore inevitably creating lack, inevitably creating injustices and imbalances.

The true way to help the earth return to a higher state – or rather transcend and flow into a higher state, for you cannot ever return to anything – is that you make an effort to transcend this mindset. You make an effort to get back to this state of Holy Innocence where you are flowing with the River of Life.

THE PURPOSE OF THE HEALING MATRIX

This, my beloved, is our entire purpose for the teaching we have given here, but especially for the invocations. This matrix, the Healing Matrix of the Song of Life, is extremely powerful and profound in terms of helping you transcend this mindset and move back towards Holy Innocence.

It is entirely possible that you can read this ritual and you may not see how profound it is. You may think it is just nursery rhymes. But my beloved, there are layers and levels and very subtle statements in this ritual that are designed by us based on our extensive experience with how we can help lifestreams overcome the duality consciousness. There are subtle keys, spiritual, alchemical keys. They may not trigger a shift in consciousness the first time, but if you keep giving this ritual, they will eventually trigger a shift in consciousness.

You will suddenly have this Aha experience where you will say: "Now I see what is going on! Now I see how I have been reacting and how I no longer want to react, how I no longer need to react." And then you realize that this is an aspect of the ego, it is a spirit you have created that is reacting this way.

For what is the key to escaping a reactionary pattern? It is that you see the pattern and then you realize: "Who is the 'you' that is seeing the pattern? Because now that I am seeing the pattern from the outside, I am no longer looking at life from inside the pattern. I am no longer looking through the pattern. And if I can step outside of the pattern that must mean that I am not the pattern. But I still see that I continue to react based on the pattern. But if I am seeing that I am reacting now, am I really the one reacting?"

"If I am not the one reacting, who is reacting? Ah, it is a spirit who is reacting because the spirit was created to react that way and can do nothing else. But since I now realize I am not the spirit, can I not then dismiss that spirit? Can I not say I do not want it anymore? Can I not make the calls to have it bound and consumed? Can I not make the calls for the masters to help me see the decision that created the spirit so that I can undo that decision by changing my mind?"

HOLDING A SPIRITUAL TORCH FOR HUMANITY

What is the greatest gift of free will? No choice you ever made can prevent you from making a different choice in the now. You can always change your mind. Of course, the fallen beings and the false teachers will hammer at you that you do not have the right to change your mind, that once you ate the forbidden fruit you are bound by that choice forever until some external savior comes to save you.

But it is not true, my beloved. And if you keep giving this Healing Matrix, there will come a point where you not only understanding this intellectually but you experience with the totality of your being that the fallen beings are lying when they say you cannot change. It is simply not true and God has given you the liberty to change your mind and to always replace a limiting choice with a liberating choice. This is liberty: When you consciously see that no matter what you have done before, no matter what situation you are facing on earth, you are at liberty to choose something higher.

Nothing on earth can take that liberty except your own choosing. And when you see this, that is when you can claim your liberty, that is when you can take your stand. You can raise your arm, and now you are carrying the Torch of Liberty for humanity as I have been carrying it for so long.

There are hundreds of thousands of people in embodiment on earth today who have it as part of their divine plan to raise the Torch of Liberty on a personal level and therefore help me hold that balance of liberty for humanity. If you are one of them then you can come to acknowledge it. If you are not one of them then that means you have another torch to hold, another spiritual flame to hold for humanity, for there are millions upon millions of people who are here to hold some spiritual flame for humanity.

So dare to see that you too can walk the spiritual path whereby you liberate yourself from the lies of the fallen beings. And as you walk that Path of the Seven Veils and beyond that towards the 144th level of consciousness, you will earn the starry crown upon your head. Not the crown of thorns, for you will transcend it and it will become the starry crown. And then you can raise up the torch of the spiritual flame that your I AM Presence wants to release on this planet so that you can be the torch bearer.

You can uphold the torch of that spiritual flame and therefore hold the balance for the transition of the earth into the golden age of Saint Germain, where spiritual liberty will be the norm and the fallen consciousness and its slavery will no longer be what is considered normal on earth. It will be considered abnormal. And the new norm will be liberty based on the Christ consciousness.

THE AGE OF MOTHER

This is the vision that I hold for each one of you: That you come to know your spiritual flame and you become the open door for it. Remember me. Dare to consider that you can walk that path. Dare to imagine, to envision, that you earn the starry crown and that whoever is your spiritual master places that starry crown on your head. And you raise your right arm and you hold high the torch of your I AM Presence and you let your light shine. As Christ said: "For the light that is set on a hill cannot be hid." And it is time in this age, this Age of Mother, to demonstrate that those who are in the mother realm can claim their right to be part of the Divine Mother and uphold a spiritual flame right while they are in embodiment.

This is your potential. This is what will shift the earth into a golden age, my beloved: That enough people uphold the torches of the spiritual light. So that everybody can now begin to look around and say: "Look how dark it is. Look how unbalanced it is."

Do you not see that this is already beginning to happen in society? But it can happen so much more the more people become consciously aware of this and dare to acknowledge: "Yes, I can uphold a spiritual torch! I am worthy. I am willing. It is my new reality. I am a spiritual being. My spirit does not have to conform to matter, it does not have to rebel against anything in matter, it does not even have to change anything in matter or produce a particular result in matter. It just has to raise up the light so that people can see more clearly."

This is liberty. And Liberty, I AM. May you be also the flame that you are.

NOTE: The invocation corresponding to this chapter is:
Song of Life 6 – Abundance

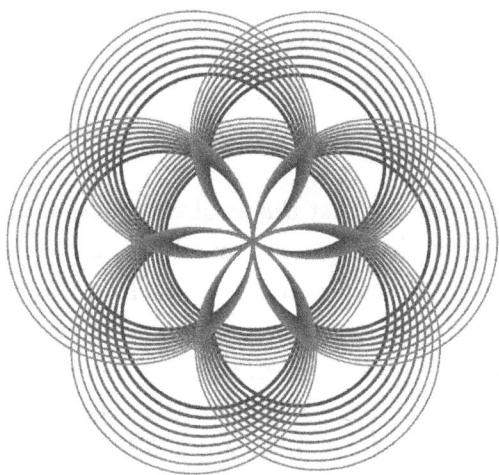

Chapter 7

LIVING IN THE FLOW OF LOVE

Lady Master Venus, I AM. I am, as some of you will know, originally from the planet Venus. I have come here to hold the balance of love for the evolutions of earth until enough people in embodiment on earth will embody unconditional love to such a degree that my presence here is no longer needed.

MILLIONS HAVE COME ON A RESCUE MISSION

Some of you will know that before my arrival on this planet, my consort, Sanat Kumara, had been here for a very long time. Some of you will know that Sanat Kumara came here because at a point in the distant past the earth had sunk to such a low level that no one was graduating from the schoolroom of earth. All were so trapped in the downward spiral created by the fallen beings that there was no output from earth. Earth had become like a black hole.

Sanat Kumara volunteered to hold the balance for the earth as a cosmic experiment to see whether it would be possible to turn around a planet that had become a dark hole, rather than letting it continue in the downward spiral until it was dissolved.

So far, the experiment has been successful in that the earth has been turned around. The inhabitants of the earth are no longer living as animals. There is indeed some sophistication and knowledge – even some self-knowledge – and there are people who ascend from earth every year. Not many, but at least the one that is the requirement for the continuation of the dispensation for earth.

What I come to give you here is a reminder that many, many millions of people on this earth have come from a different realm. When Sanat Kumara descended originally, he was accompanied by 144,000 lifestreams from Venus. But after they had been successful in turning the earth around and starting a very tentative upward spiral, many millions of lifestreams have come to earth from other planetary systems, even from other star systems and galaxies. These many people came here because they wanted to be part of the experiment to see whether a dark star could be turned into Freedom's Star.

Many of the lifestreams who volunteered to come here had reached a certain level of consciousness at their original growth place. Yet they obviously had not ascended from that place, just as the 144,000 that originally came from Venus had not ascended at the time they came. For you see, had they been ascended masters in embodiment, what would be the point in the experiment?

HOW TO TURN AROUND A PLANET

We who are ascended have the power to descend into embodiment and instantly turn around a planet, but how will that help the people, the lifestreams, embodying on that planet? This will only reinforce the false image given through several religions, including Christianity, that there is only one person that can be God on earth. And this will not turn around a planet. For what will turn around a planet is when many people realize that God is in them and they are the open doors whereby God can express itself on this planet. This then will turn around a planet.

So, the 144,000 from Venus had not ascended and they came to set forth an example that even on this dark star of earth it is possible to start the upward spiral leading towards the ascension. The millions of others, who have come from other systems, have also come in the unascended state, and they have come to demonstrate that it is possible to embody here and submit to the death consciousness and yet still retain that inner momentum, that inner memory, that inner knowing that there is more to life than what you see on earth, and that by striving for it you can raise your consciousness until you become an open door for that which is more.

So then, the story of Sanat Kumara has relevance not only to the 144,000 but to the millions of others who have descended on earth. For truly, those who descended on earth after Sanat Kumara came all descended through his office. And thus, they are naturally at inner levels familiar with Sanat Kumara. They know the name. They know what Venus is the Love Star.

THE IMPORTANCE OF LOVE

By the way, my beloved, why do you think that so many cultures around the world associate the planet Venus with love? Surely, it is a visible planet in the sky and it looks like a star, but why associate it with love? Almost every culture does this, even cultures that had no interaction at the physical level.

You know, then, the reason is that there are so many that have come through the office of the Love Star and embodied here to help raise this planet and retain the inner memory that Venus holds the spiritual balance and the focus of love for earth.

Love then is the key, for it was the love from Venus that turned earth around. And it is only love that will carry earth to her ascension point.

There are many other God qualities that are part of this upward spiral, but only love can carry it through to its ultimate conclusion. Thus, I come to give you the sense that love is a flow, an upward flow. Love is not something static, as many people on earth see love as something static, for they have come to believe in the fallen angels and their portrayal of love as conditional. You must live up to conditions and then you will receive love from God forever and ever. But there is no forever and ever.

There is no standstill anywhere in the world of form, for the world of form is, as the Maha Chohan has explained, an upward spiral of the flow of the Holy Spirit, the River of Life. The River of Life is the River of Love on earth for it is through love that you can tune in to the River of Life of the entire universe. The River of Life of the entire universe is a blending of all God qualities. But on earth, as I said, the key to the turning around of the downward spiral was the love from Venus, and thus love is still the key for tuning in to the flow of life on earth, and it will remain so until the earth ascends.

THREE TYPES OF LIFESTREAMS

Thus, I come to give you this gift of another invocation to the Flow of Love whereby you may tune in to this Flow of Love that I AM, that Sanat Kumara is, that those on Venus are, and that we hold for earth. We hold that balance of the Flow of Love, the ever-flowing, ever-transcending love that will not accept any condition as permanent, any condition as unchangeable, for we realize that all can be transformed, all can be consumed by the ongoing, never-stopping flow of love.

Nothing on earth can stop the flow of love except, of course, free will. For if there are not enough people on earth who will be the open doors for the flow of love, then love will be stopped. And thus, the big question is: Can the lifestreams on earth become the open doors for love so that they themselves can bring forth enough love to maintain and even increase an upward momentum, the upward spiral of this planet?

For so far, you understand that this upward spiral was created by those who descended here, who took on the density of this planet and still managed to ascend. But you see, there are three main categories of lifestreams on this planet:

1. There are those who have descended voluntarily from a different realm. They came here not because they karmically had to come here, but because they volunteered to come here.

2. Then there are those who fell here because they misused their opportunity on another planet. When that planet ascended they could no longer hold on and so they fell to this dark star of earth because the vibrations on earth corresponded to their consciousness.

3. But the third and most important category on earth are those lifestreams who embodied here as new innocent lifestreams. These are the ones who were the Holy Innocents.

You may know that before the fall on earth there were several waves of these lifestreams who embodied here and who ascended, and who therefore created an upward spiral. But then, at some point, the fall happened, and after that point the dark lifestreams from other planets were allowed to embody here and they gradually created a downward spiral that, as I said, threatened the dissolution of the entire planetary body.

At this point, when the earth was at a low point, those who were the original lifestreams – who had been part of taking this planet into the downward spiral – were still, most of them, in embodiment here. You must understand that even if the earth had been dissolved, these lifestreams, the original innocent ones, would not have been dissolved in the ritual of the second death. Those who were the fallen beings, who had taken earth further into the downward spiral, many of those would have been dissolved in the second death. But the original ones would not. They would have had to go to another planet and receive further opportunities to raise their consciousness.

But it was determined that we would attempt to give them that opportunity here on earth. And the condition is, of course, that we who have come from other realms, whether Venus or other planets, we cannot bring the earth to the ascension point. We can turn around the downward pull that was created by the fallen beings, for we are allowed to hold the balance for what the fallen beings have done. We can set an example so that those who were the innocent lifestreams on earth can follow that example, but we cannot carry the earth to the ascension, for the ascension or descension of the earth does not depend on the fallen beings or those who have volunteered to come here. It depends exclusively on those who were the original Holy Innocents, those for whom the earth was their first opportunity to embody in the material universe.

So the question really is: Can those who are the original lifestreams be awakened so that they become the open doors for the flow of life? And that, of course, depends very much on the example set by those who have descended. And thus, I will address those who have descended.

THE KEY TO YOUR ASCENSION

You will know in your innermost being that the key to your ascension and the key to the fulfillment of your mission on earth is love, nothing but love. This presents a delicate challenge, for many of you who volunteered to come to earth came here with a sense that something had gone wrong on earth, that there was something that needed to be corrected, that you needed to come here to do something, to correct something, to compensate for something. And while this is not incorrect, you must understand that this was the mindset that brought you to earth but it will not carry you to your ascension from earth.

You cannot ascend from earth with the same mindset with which you descended to earth. This is equally true of the fallen beings who fell here as it is for those who volunteered to come here. There are those who volunteered to come here and who have fallen prey to the illusion of the fallen angels, namely that the condition on earth is because there is a flaw in God's design relating to free will.

You, of course, need to escape that illusion before you can ascend. But you also need to escape the image that you had when you volunteered to come here, namely that you are here to do something, to correct something, or that you are here to save the earth. For you see, you are not here to save the earth—only those who are the original lifestreams can do this. All you can do is set an example of a being who is the open door for the ever-flowing, ever-transcending stream of love. This is your only possibility for fulfilling your mission.

Thus you see, you were not ascended when you came to earth. What does this mean? Why had you not ascended? There is only way to not ascended and that is to maintain some level of illusion based on the consciousness of separation. What is the key to ascending? It is to let go of these spirits, these ghosts, that spring from separation until you let go of the last ghost, and then you can ascend.

Certainly, some of those spirits that you need to let go of is the idea that you are here to do something, that you have the power to raise the earth—because you do not, as I have explained. Only those who are the original lifestreams can bring the earth to the ascension point. They can do so only when they become the open doors for the power of God to stream through them. You too can become an open door for the power of God to stream through you while you are in embodiment, but this will not be enough to bring the earth to the ascension point. It has been enough to bring the earth into a positive spiral, but the spiral has really only been created because some among the original lifestreams of earth responded to the example given by Sanat Kumara, by Gautama, by Maitreya and other ascended masters.

IMMERSE YOURSELF IN THE FLOW OF LOVE

Are there some among the original lifestreams who have ascended? Yes. Not many, but some. Yet most of the beings who have ascended from earth were beings who came from elsewhere. Yet I must tell you that we are in an age – we are in a cosmic cycle – where it is time that many more of those who descended voluntarily to earth reach their ascension point. And you can do so only by letting go of whatever image you had when you first descended here, by completely letting go of it and surrendering yourself into, immersing yourself into, the flow of love.

You are not here to attain specific, outer, physical results. You are here to be an open door for love so that you increase the light on this planet, whereby the original lifestreams of earth can make enlightened choices. It is their choices that determine the fate of the earth, not your choices. Your choices can serve as an example, but only if you let go of the mindset that there is a particular physical outcome that must be manifest and that you are here to manifest it.

You must surrender into the flow of love where you see yourself only as an open door for love, and you realize there is only one reason for you being here, and that is to be that open door for that which is more, that which is forever more and will never stop becoming more. Thus, any image you have of yourself must be surrendered before you can become more than that image, for otherwise that image will hold you back and you will no longer be the open door for love. And thus, you will no longer raise the earth.

There are actually some who volunteered to come here with the best of intentions, who have closed their beings – their chakras – so that they are no longer open doors and they are now helping to pull the earth down. And this is, of course, not what we desire to see happen.

This is indeed one of the reasons why we of the Lady Masters have decided to give this matrix, this Healing Matrix of the Song of Life, so that those who were the volunteers who came here can be healed of whatever wounds and illusions they have taken on so that they can ascend. But of course, the matrix is equally valid for the original lifestreams on earth who can also be healed and thereby win their ascension. And it can equally be used by those who fell here, who can also use this to heal themselves if they are willing, although it is predictable that a certain percentage of them will not be willing and must therefore be taken to other planets or taken to the second death after the sojourn on this earth.

CUTTING TIES WITH FALLEN BEINGS

You will see, of course, that there are those who will not stop attacking, criticizing, mocking the innocent lifestreams on earth or mocking those who volunteered to come here. Do you not see that those who volunteered to come here have given an opportunity to the fallen lifestreams that they may remain in embodiment, that they may remain in the illusion of having control of this planet? But do you think the fallen lifestreams have any sense of gratitude for this? Nay. For they see themselves as being in competition with those who volunteered.

Many of you who are the volunteers have seen this in your own lifestreams, for many of you have volunteered – as another expression of your desire to serve – you have volunteered to embody in close, personal relationships with those who fell here, those who are trapped in the fallen consciousness. You have given them an opportunity that they might see your example, that you are driven by love, that your relationship to God is based on love and not fear, that you do not have a desire to control others, that you do not have a sense of ownership over other people, that you do not have a desire to put them down, to criticize and to mock them, and to tear down those who will not be controlled by you.

You have volunteered in many cases to have such beings as parents, as children, as spouses, as bosses, as co-workers. You have given them opportunity after opportunity, and at this time I tell you that you need to let go of any attachment you might have to saving those in the fallen consciousness. Some of them cannot be saved, at least not here on earth. They must either be taken somewhere else or be taken to the Court of the Sacred Fire and taken to the second death. This is not your decision to make. It is their decision.

But you must let go of the desire to save such lifestreams, for if you tie yourself to them you cannot enter your personal ascension spiral, and thus you cannot help raise the earth to a higher level. It is time for the many among the 144,000 from Venus, and among the millions more who have come from other systems, to let go of your attachments to particular lifestreams on earth, especially those in the fallen consciousness.

A RUBY RAY FOCUS IN YOUR HEART

If you will tune in, you will see very simply who they are, for you have the ability. Every single lifestream who volunteered to come here, who have come through the office of Sanat Kumara, you were given a gift before you descended to this earth, and that is that Sanat Kumara himself placed a focus of the flame of love that we have called the Ruby Ray in your heart. This focus is a flame that burns, and it burns with a flame of unconditional love. If you will make the effort, as we have given you these tools of the Healing Matrix, you can come back into a conscious contact and conscious attunement with that flame of love. And therefore, you can know that love is beyond the conditions found on earth. Love is unconditional, as we might say, for it is truly beyond conditions.

When you know this, when you have this frame of reference in your heart, you will know and you will be able to instantly feel where there are those on earth who mock unconditional love, who seek to tear it down, who seek to argue against it, who seek to reject it and make you feel rejected for offering it to them. They hold on to the image of the angry, judgmental God in the sky whose love is portrayed as being conditional.

When you have attunement with the Ruby Ray focus in your own heart, you will know that love, true love, is beyond conditions – any conditions – on earth. Venusian love is beyond any conditions created by the fallen consciousness on earth. Thus, you will be able to identify those close to you who do not have that focus in their hearts, because those who fell here – even the original lifestreams here – do not have that focus because they did not pass through the office of Sanat Kumara before they came into embodiment on earth.

Thus, you will know, when you recognize those who do not have the focus of unconditional love, that it is not your job to save them. It is in many cases your voluntary job to give them opportunity after opportunity to encounter the unconditional love in your heart. But there comes a point when it is time to say: "Enough is enough. I will move on in the ongoing flow of the River of Life, the River of Love that is constantly transcending itself, for I will no longer adapt myself to these people so that I can continue to be associated with them and give them an opportunity to sense my love. I will flow with the flow of love and therefore I will transcend myself to the point I simply cannot be bothered by adapting to these people. Thus, if they are spun out of my circle of influence so be it, for it is their decision that spins them out. For I simply desire to move on with the River of Love that is the very core of my being here on earth, for it is through this flame that I embodied on this planet."

"And I am true to that original flame from Sanat Kumara because I am loyal to Sanat Kumara, and I want to see Sanat Kumara have the victory of earth. And therefore, I will contribute to that victory the only way I can, by multiplying the focus of the ruby ray in my heart, which gives me the strength and the power to flow with the ever-transcending flow of love so that I will not be stuck here. I will not stay in an adaptation to those who mock love and who put it down. I will simply transcend myself and transcend them if they will not follow me in self-transcendence."

"Thus, let this be my decision to be who I am, and they must decide who they want to be at this moment: whether they will stay where they are or come up higher. That is the decision I leave to them. But as for me, I will to my own self be true and thus I cannot be false to any man. I must be true to who I am and I must say: 'I am moving on. Your decision to move on is yours. But I have made mine. I remain true to that decision.' And thus I use this Healing Matrix to heal all attachments, all wounds that make me think I have to keep paying attention to those who mock the most precious flame that I brought to this planet, the flame of unconditional love that is the Ruby Ray."

THE LASER BEAM OF THE RUBY RAY

Do you not see that ruby is the color that is often associated with a laser beam? What is a laser beam? It is one where the light is completely coherent, for there is no division in the light. And how can there be no division in the light? Only when there are no conditions. For the only thing that divides is the conditions you create when you take on the serpentine mindset and think you are now a God who can define the conditions for what is good and the conditions for what is evil.

This is the fallen ones' mindset. This is a mindset you can transcend by tuning in to the Ruby Ray whereby you transcend all need to judge, all need to have a dualistic standard of right and wrong, good and evil, that you apply to others. You are simply the open door for love. You are not in your mind deciding or judging who is worthy to receive that love for you allow it to flow as love wants to flow.

You allow the Holy Spirit to blow where it listeth and you allow unconditional love to seek to set people free from their conditions by challenging those conditions or by giving them an example of how to live beyond conditions.

This is your opportunity. This Healing Matrix is a supreme opportunity for all lifestreams on earth who are willing to move on in the eternal flow of ever-transcending, unconditional love, the flow that I AM, the flow that Sanat Kumara is, the flow that we have opened for the earth and continue to hold open. Thus, join us in that flow and be all that you came here to be.

*NOTE: The invocation corresponding to this chapter is:
Song of Life 7 – Loving Flow*

Chapter 8

KNOWING YOURSELF AS GOD KNOWS YOU

Omega, I AM. But which Omega am I? For there is a Central Sun in the etheric realm of your unascended sphere. There is a Central Sun in each of the ascended spheres. And there is, of course, the ultimate Central Sun in the first sphere. Yet truly, does it matter? For each of the Central Suns serves as the cosmic gate that can open up the veil of form and expose the formless God, and thus help you connect to the formless God that is your source.

THE DIVINE POLARITY

You may see that we are two beings, Alpha and Omega, holding the masculine-feminine balance in the Central Sun. Yet Alpha is not the ultimate God. Alpha is a representative of God that exists only in polarity with Omega. It is only the formless God who has no polarity, who needs no polarity.

Thus you see, in the world of form everything exists in a polarity between the expanding and the contracting force, the yin and the yang, the masculine and feminine, the Alpha and Omega, whatever you want to call it. There is always a polarity.

Thus, we can say that the entire world of form is also in a polarity with the formless Creator. And thus, in that polarity the formless Creator represents the masculine and the world of form represents the feminine. Yet take note that in the world of form, nothing can exist without its opposite polarity. Masculine cannot exist within feminine.

But the one Creator who is beyond form can indeed exist without its polarity. The Creator did exist before the world of form was created. There was no need for the Creator to create a world of form in order to create itself. But when your Creator did decide to create, your Creator voluntarily placed itself in a polarity with its own creation. Thus, one can say that the Creator, by embedding its own Being in the world of form, has voluntarily placed itself in a polarity that it cannot walk away from because if it did the world of form and all self-aware extensions of the Creator would cease to exist.

One can say that by choice the Creator cannot exist without its polarity, although the Creator could indeed exist, but the world of form could not. Of course, because the Creator does not want to dissolve its own creation, it will stay in this polarity until the self-aware extensions of the Creator have reached the Creator consciousness.

These are the realities that you learn as you travel to the retreats of the ascended masters at various levels. We are giving you these teachings in the physical so that you might ponder them. Not that we ask you to believe them with the outer, intellectual mind. We ask you to meditate upon them until you experience within your own hearts their reality.

YOU CAN EXPERIENCE THE FORMLESS GOD

This messenger has described how he was once taken to the Central Sun and experienced the central hall with the great white pillars, with the throne of Alpha and Omega, the figure-eight flow between us, and the nexus of the figure-eight opening up to the formless God. This is an experience that all of you can have for you are all self-aware extensions of the Creator. But are you willing to have that experience? Are you willing to experience the formless Creator, which will then become the ultimate frame of reference, and which will then demonstrate to you that there is nothing in the world of form that has ultimate reality or permanence—and therefore, it has no ultimate importance?

Therefore, is it really worth it to take things so personally? For I assure you that when you are in the Central Sun you gain an entirely different perspective on life on planet earth. You can sit there on the white cube and look out over the vastness of this material universe. You can see how many millions of galaxies, millions of suns, millions of solar systems, millions of planets there are. You can see that there are so many with intelligent, self-aware life, and the vast majority of them are in an upward spiral, the River of Life, the Holy Spirit.

But there are some that are behind that upward flow, that have set themselves apart, that are lagging behind. And when you realize that earth is such a planet, is there really anything one earth that has ultimate importance? Is there really anything that has greater importance than your growth in consciousness and your growth towards the ascension where you can leave this planet behind permanently, for you have done what you came here to do: You have been the open door for love, as Venus so beautifully explained?

THE REASON FOR THE PUTTING DOWN OF WOMEN

The fallen beings want to trap you into thinking that you cannot be the Christ until certain outer conditions are fulfilled. They want you to think that you cannot be in embodiment on earth and be in a polarity with your God, that you cannot accept yourself as the Divine Mother in embodiment on earth—the Divine Mother that is always in the correct polarity with the Divine Father, that is always one with the Father. This is what they do not want to happen. They do not want you to accept that you are a representative of the Divine Mother on earth and that you are in a polarity with the formless God whereby the power of that formless God can stream through you.

Thus, they have – now for thousands upon thousands of years of recorded history, but even longer – put down the feminine, both the divine feminine and the embodied feminine. Look at the intense accusations and humiliations against women on this planet. Look at the fact that in some countries daughters are considered worthless and even sold as property, sold into sex slavery, or killed because you do not want another mouth to feed.

This is not only disrespect for the Divine Mother, it is hatred of the mother. And this is a force that has been around on this planet since the original fallen beings came here in the beginning. And they have continued ever since to put down the Mother, to put down the feminine, for they will not see themselves as part of the Divine Feminine.

THE QUEST FOR POWER

They lust after ultimate power and they believe that they should be as gods who do not need to submit into a polarity with the

Divine Father in order to gain power. They should be able to have power on their own without being in such a polarity. This is the pride and the arrogance of those who think they have become a law onto themselves, being so deceived by the serpentine mind that they think they can define reality and that the entire universe, even God, will comply with their definition.

When you are in the Central Sun you can see how tiny is their sphere of influence on a planet like earth, how insignificant it is compared to the totality of the material universe and the upward flow of the Holy Spirit. You can see that were it not for the fact that many, both ascended and non-ascended lifestreams, are holding the balance for these fallen beings, they would long ago have been spun off—not only spun off earth but spun out of the material universe, either going to the astral realm or going to the second death.

Truly, part of the reason why planet earth has been allowed to lag behind for so long is to give many of these fallen lifestreams another opportunity. But as Venus said, it is time for you to realize that it is no longer your job to give them this opportunity and therefore leave it up to their own choices whether they will learn from example or whether they will continue to believe that they have the power to define reality and unreality.

For I can assure you that when you are in the Central Sun you see clearly what is reality, and you see that almost everything on earth is unreality. And thus, of course, you know that you carry with you that frame of reference that makes you realize that you do not need to adapt or submit to anything on earth for you are a free-born spirit. You are a free-born self. Your role is not to come here to submit. But neither is it your role to come here and rebel. For whether you submit to the fallen beings or rebel against them, you are trapped in the net of reacting to them.

THE SERPENTINE DECEPTION

Now you see, why is this such a deception? Why is it so easy for people to fall for the serpentine lie? What does the serpentine lie actually say? It says: "You are not part of the Divine Feminine. You are a self-sufficient being who can exist on its own. You do not need the Divine Father for you can become as a god who can define your own reality." This is the surface deception.

But the deeper reality is that when you let go of your polarity with the formless God, what happens? You violate the first two commandments: "Thou shalt have no other Gods before me. Thou shalt not take onto thyself any graven image." You now put a "god" from the world of form before the formless God and you worship a graven image of that god of form. And that graven image is created by the fallen beings whereby you indirectly worship and submit to them.

You cannot be a self-sufficient being when you are unascended. This is impossible. You can only fulfill your reason for being, you can only ascend, by seeing yourself in a correct polarity with the formless God, which is why Jesus said: "I and my Father are one. I can of my own self do nothing. The Father within me, he doeth the work."

When you acknowledge that you are part of the Divine Feminine and that you are in a polarity with the formless masculine, then you can fulfill your reason for being. And then you will not be deceived by the fallen beings for you will carry with you, even in your waking awareness, the ability to discern and see their unreality, expose it for what it is and know that it has no power over you.

EVERY WOUND CAN BE HEALED

What have we done with this Healing Matrix of the Song of Life? We have given you teachings and practical tools that can heal every wound, every burden, every illusion you have received while in embodiment in this unascended sphere. Literally, there is nothing that cannot be healed if you are willing to use these teachings and these tools to bring yourself back into alignment, so that you are in a true polarity where you know you are the Divine Feminine in complete polarity and oneness with the Divine Masculine.

The Divine Masculine is represented to you in the unascended sphere by the ascended masters in the sphere right above you, but also in the cosmic hierarchy that reaches all the way to the Central Sun—and the Central Sun, and the Central Sun, and the ultimate Central Sun.

You are in that kind of polarity between the unascended sphere and the ascended realm. But you are still in a polarity between the world of form and the formless Creator. And this is why you can know that you never need to submit or adapt to any form, especially not in the unascended sphere. You can continue to transcend any form until you reach the Creator consciousness.

We have given you these tools. We have imbedded many secret, esoteric teachings within them. We have encoded certain codes of numbers. You may try to decode them if you like, but really: Be careful that you do not become caught in the pride of the intellect of wanting to decode and understand everything. For truly, for this ritual to be most effective, you need to give it as a little child with a beginner's mind, with the innocence of the child. That will ensure the greatest effect. And you have to ask yourself: "Do I want to understand or do I want to transcend?" For you cannot transcend as a separate observer observing a separate object. You can ascend only by becoming one with, by seeing yourself in polarity with.

STOP RESISTING THE FLOW

Thus, resistance is futile for nothing can in the long run resist the ascending movement of the River of Life. This you can see from the Central Sun more clearly than anywhere in the unascended realm. When you are in that Central Sun, you know that the immensity of the universe is such that no single being, no single planet, not even a single galaxy can withstand it.

O what a beautiful Song of Life you hear when you sit on the White Cube in the Central Sun and you attune your inner ear to what has been called the music of the spheres. What an incredible performance you see unfolding before you as you actually experience with all of your higher senses this incredible tapestry of life, this incredible ballet, this incredible symphony, this incredible dance. What incredible, translucent beauty, such beauty as could never be seen from any vantage point from the unascended sphere. But you can get a glimpse of it, get a feel for it, when you attune yourself to the Song of Life. And we have given you the ultimate tool that has ever been released in the physical for attuning yourself to the Song of Life. The decision on how to use it is yours.

I, Omega, love you with an infinite, unconditional love regardless of what you decide. But I would much prefer that you would decide to join the upward spiral so that you will come to the point of healing and purity that allows you to travel even in your conscious awareness to the Central Sun. That you may stand before the throne of Alpha and myself and you may feel, you may experience, how we give you that Pearl of Great Price that contains your divine individuality, the price that it is worth it to sell everything that thou hast in order to attain it, for nothing in the world of form can be more precious to you than the gift of your divine individuality.

That individuality I love, and I long to come to the point where I see you able to love that divine individuality before the human, separate individuality that you have so far considered to be yourself. You are infinitely more than a human self. I desire you to know that more as I know that more. Truly, therefore, use the tools we have given that you may know yourself as I know you.

NOTE: The invocation corresponding to this chapter is: Song of Life 8 – Omega Flow

Part Two

Song of Life
Invocations

NOTE: If you want to attain a very powerful healing effect, give all eight invocations in one setting, which will take about two hours. When you do this, you do not need to give the individual preamble and sealing for each invocation. Use the following preamble when you start, and after you finish give the general sealing that is printed at the end of Part Two.

GENERAL PREAMBLE:

In the name I AM THAT I AM, Jesus Christ, I call to all representatives of the Divine Mother, especially Maraytaii, Nada, Kuan Yin, Mother Mary, Portia, Liberty, Venus and Omega for the healing of my four lower bodies, for the healing of all imbalanced conditions in my life and for the physical manifestation of the perfect health and abundant wealth needed for the fulfillment of my Divine plan. I call forth the transcendence of all imbalances, including...

[Make personal calls.]

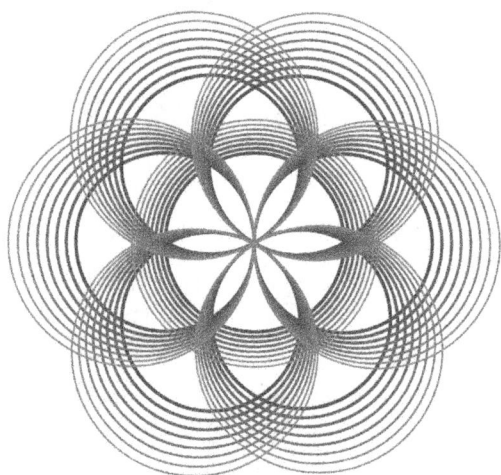

Song of Life 1

A NEW IDENTITY

In the name I AM THAT I AM, Jesus Christ, I call to all representatives of the Divine Mother, especially Maraytaii and Mother Mary, for the healing of my four lower bodies, especially for the transfiguration of my identity body, my sense of self. I call forth the transcendence of all illusions of a separate self, including...

[Make personal calls.]

When Father-Mother are as One,
I see the rising of the Son.
My Christic balance is the key,
extremes they cannot capture me.

When I am centered in the One,
my inner balance I have won.
My I AM Presence now can do,
all that it wants through Conscious You.

When I have balanced Yang and Yin,
the victory of Christ I win.
As Mara's demons I transcend,
the eightfold path I do ascend.

When I complete the sacred quest,
fulfilling every subtle test.
With Jesus I the ghost release,
Gautama Buddha shows me peace.

When with Maitreya I am free,
Sanat Kumara greeting me.
Alpha-Omega are now one,
I am with them in Central Sun.

When nexus of their figure-eight,
opens up the cosmic gate.
With my Creator I can be,
I AM in true polarity.

When I return to planet earth,
a brand new Self is given birth.
I know now what for all is best,
the Will of God is manifest.

1. I am a being of light

1. I see now with the single eye,
there's more to what we call the "I."
For I AM come from Sacred light,
I have descended from great height.

O Cosmic Mother, sound the gong,
that calls me home where I belong.
I know you love me tenderly,
and in that knowing I am free.

Maraytaii, I resonate
with song that opens cosmic gate.
Your melody makes me vibrate
my sense of self I recreate.

2. I come from out the cosmic womb,
and thus I shatter human tomb.
For I am born a Spirit Spark,
I come to light up what is dark.

O Cosmic Mother, hold me tight,
I resonate with your own light.
Your music purifies my heart,
your love to all I do impart.

Maraytaii, I resonate
with song that opens cosmic gate.
Your melody makes me vibrate
my sense of self I recreate.

3. Creator's Being gave me birth,
a child of God's own cosmic mirth.
From love I came, to love I go,
transcending self in Mother's flow.

O Cosmic Mother, we are one,
your heart is like a blazing sun.
My being can but amplify,
the sacred sound you magnify.

**Maraytaii, I resonate
with song that opens cosmic gate.
Your melody makes me vibrate
my sense of self I recreate.**

4. I start as point in firmament,
I seek a self that's permanent,
by always seeking what is more,
transcending what I was before.

O Cosmic Mother, I now hear,
the subtle sound of Sacred Sphere.
As I attune to Cosmic Hum,
the lesser self I overcome.

**Maraytaii, I resonate
with song that opens cosmic gate.
Your melody makes me vibrate
my sense of self I recreate.**

5. I am at heart awareness pure,
my sense of self yet immature.
Yet my potential is to be
as God who first created me.

O Cosmic Mother, take me home,
I am in sync with Sacred OM,
The sound of sounds will raise me up,
so only light is in my cup.

**Maraytaii, I resonate
with song that opens cosmic gate.
Your melody makes me vibrate
my sense of self I recreate.**

6. And when I flow with life's own stream,
I help fulfill Creator's dream,
to bring the self from single point,
to where He can a God anoint.

O Cosmic Mother, I will be,
a part of cosmic symphony.
All that I AM, an instrument,
for sound that is from heaven sent.

**Maraytaii, I resonate
with song that opens cosmic gate.
Your melody makes me vibrate
my sense of self I recreate.**

7. But though the goal is firmly set,
the journey isn't over yet.
The journey is what I enjoy,
and nothing can my growth destroy.

O Cosmic Mother, I now call,
to enter sacred music hall.
I will be part of life's ascent,
towards the starry firmament.

Maraytaii, I resonate
with song that opens cosmic gate.
Your melody makes me vibrate
my sense of self I recreate.

8. And as I see my life unfold,
I come to see design so bold,
For truly, as I self-transcend,
to progress mine there is no end.

O Cosmic Mother, tune my strings,
my total being with you sings.
Your song I now reverberate,
as cosmic love I celebrate.

Maraytaii, I resonate
with song that opens cosmic gate.
Your melody makes me vibrate
my sense of self I recreate.

9. All consciousness a flowing stream,
the self like sun's translucent gleam.
My self-awareness is God's gift,
it is my role the self to shift.

O Cosmic Mother, I love you,
your love song keeps me ever true.
You fill me with your sacred tone,
and thus I never feel alone.

**Maraytaii, I resonate
with song that opens cosmic gate.
Your melody makes me vibrate
my sense of self I recreate.**

2. Awakening from illusion

1. In heart of hearts I do so long,
for a real sense that I belong.
Which proves I did not come from dust,
for finding meaning is a must.

O Cosmic Mother, sound the gong,
that calls me home where I belong.
I know you love me tenderly,
and in that knowing I am free.

**Maraytaii, I resonate
with song that opens cosmic gate.
Your melody makes me vibrate
my sense of self I recreate.**

2. The self new orbit has begun,
like planet round a central sun.
The I AM Presence is my home,
around it I am free to roam.

O Cosmic Mother, hold me tight,
I resonate with your own light.
Your music purifies my heart,
your love to all I do impart.

Maraytaii, I resonate
with song that opens cosmic gate.
Your melody makes me vibrate
my sense of self I recreate.

3. Yet if I go too far astray,
I can be lost in matter's fray.
Forgetting source from whence I came,
and thinking I am not the same.

O Cosmic Mother, we are one,
your heart is like a blazing sun.
My being can but amplify,
the sacred sound you magnify.

Maraytaii, I resonate
with song that opens cosmic gate.
Your melody makes me vibrate
my sense of self I recreate.

4. When I forget, I do give birth,
to a new self that's born from earth.
And through its filter I now see,
thinking this is really me.

O Cosmic Mother, I now hear,
the subtle sound of Sacred Sphere.
As I attune to Cosmic Hum,
the lesser self I overcome.

Maraytaii, I resonate
with song that opens cosmic gate.
Your melody makes me vibrate
my sense of self I recreate.

5. Yet this forgetting is all part,
of God's unfolding work of art.
Through separate self I do receive,
temptation serpent gave to Eve.

O Cosmic Mother, take me home,
I am in sync with Sacred OM,
The sound of sounds will raise me up,
so only light is in my cup.

Maraytaii, I resonate
with song that opens cosmic gate.
Your melody makes me vibrate
my sense of self I recreate.

6. The serpent is the fallen lot,
who in past spheres the self forgot.
And now they seek to pull us in,
to follow them in downward spin.

O Cosmic Mother, I will be,
a part of cosmic symphony.
All that I AM, an instrument,
for sound that is from heaven sent.

Maraytaii, I resonate
with song that opens cosmic gate.
Your melody makes me vibrate
my sense of self I recreate.

7. They seek to make us all believe,
the world is just as they perceive.
They tell us we cannot retreat,
because of fruit that we did eat.

O Cosmic Mother, I now call,
to enter sacred music hall.
I will be part of life's ascent,
towards the starry firmament.

Maraytaii, I resonate
with song that opens cosmic gate.
Your melody makes me vibrate
my sense of self I recreate.

8. Yet now I see this is a lie,
that seems so real to dual eye.
Regardless of what I did choose,
the right to change, I cannot lose.

O Cosmic Mother, tune my strings,
my total being with you sings.
Your song I now reverberate,
as cosmic love I celebrate.

Maraytaii, I resonate
with song that opens cosmic gate.
Your melody makes me vibrate
my sense of self I recreate.

9. There is no doubt I can return,
as soon as lesson I do learn.
I now see through the serpent's plot,
a god the separate self is not.

O Cosmic Mother, I love you,
your love song keeps me ever true.
You fill me with your sacred tone,
and thus I never feel alone.

Maraytaii, I resonate
with song that opens cosmic gate.
Your melody makes me vibrate
my sense of self I recreate.

3. I see that the world is unreal

1. What is it then, this fleeting self?
It is not something "off the shelf."
For I am truly quite unique,
and frankly also "magnifique."

O Cosmic Mother, sound the gong,
that calls me home where I belong.
I know you love me tenderly,
and in that knowing I am free.

Maraytaii, I resonate
with song that opens cosmic gate.
Your melody makes me vibrate
my sense of self I recreate.

2. And thus in love I do embrace,
that I am now in time and space.
For I know this is where I win,
the victory of Christ within.

O Cosmic Mother, hold me tight,
I resonate with your own light.
Your music purifies my heart,
your love to all I do impart.

Maraytaii, I resonate
with song that opens cosmic gate.
Your melody makes me vibrate
my sense of self I recreate.

3. For even here on planet earth,
the Christ within is given birth.
My Christ potentiality,
to go beyond duality.

O Cosmic Mother, we are one,
your heart is like a blazing sun.
My being can but amplify,
the sacred sound you magnify.

**Maraytaii, I resonate
with song that opens cosmic gate.
Your melody makes me vibrate
my sense of self I recreate.**

4. I shatter consciousness of death,
as I partake of sacred breath.
The matter world is but a stage,
for turning me into a sage.

O Cosmic Mother, I now hear,
the subtle sound of Sacred Sphere.
As I attune to Cosmic Hum,
the lesser self I overcome.

**Maraytaii, I resonate
with song that opens cosmic gate.
Your melody makes me vibrate
my sense of self I recreate.**

5. The inner Christ does now reveal,
that nothing here is truly real.
However solid it may seem,
this world is a collective dream.

O Cosmic Mother, take me home,
I am in sync with Sacred OM,
The sound of sounds will raise me up,
so only light is in my cup.

Maraytaii, I resonate
with song that opens cosmic gate.
Your melody makes me vibrate
my sense of self I recreate.

6. The world is what we make it; true,
but when we higher dream pursue,
the Ma-ter light will then comply,
as we our vision purify.

O Cosmic Mother, I will be,
a part of cosmic symphony.
All that I AM, an instrument,
for sound that is from heaven sent.

Maraytaii, I resonate
with song that opens cosmic gate.
Your melody makes me vibrate
my sense of self I recreate.

7. And thus our self-made lack and strife,
is not all that there is to life.
And now with Christ I take a stand,
I seek to help all understand.

O Cosmic Mother, I now call,
to enter sacred music hall.
I will be part of life's ascent,
towards the starry firmament.

**Maraytaii, I resonate
with song that opens cosmic gate.
Your melody makes me vibrate
my sense of self I recreate.**

8. To God's abundance I wake up,
the love of Christ now fills my cup.
The bubbling joy o'erflows my heart,
I now accept a fresh new start.

O Cosmic Mother, tune my strings,
my total being with you sings.
Your song I now reverberate,
as cosmic love I celebrate.

**Maraytaii, I resonate
with song that opens cosmic gate.
Your melody makes me vibrate
my sense of self I recreate.**

9. My true potential I accept,
I am at heart a real adept.
For I am here to show all men,
that Christ through me has come again.

O Cosmic Mother, I love you,
your love song keeps me ever true.
You fill me with your sacred tone,
and thus I never feel alone.

**Maraytaii, I resonate
with song that opens cosmic gate.
Your melody makes me vibrate
my sense of self I recreate.**

4. The victory of Christ I win

1. I see that every circumstance
is part of life's intriguing dance.
It's all an opportunity,
from ancient karma to be free.

O Cosmic Mother, sound the gong,
that calls me home where I belong.
I know you love me tenderly,
and in that knowing I am free.

**Maraytaii, I resonate
with song that opens cosmic gate.
Your melody makes me vibrate
my sense of self I recreate.**

2. My expectations I let go,
my only purpose is to grow.
When my reactions I control,
I will fulfill my highest role.

O Cosmic Mother, hold me tight,
I resonate with your own light.
Your music purifies my heart,
your love to all I do impart.

**Maraytaii, I resonate
with song that opens cosmic gate.
Your melody makes me vibrate
my sense of self I recreate.**

3. To outcome I am not attached,
and thus the devil is dispatched.
For worldly prince cannot fool me,
with single eye of Christ I see.

O Cosmic Mother, we are one,
your heart is like a blazing sun.
My being can but amplify,
the sacred sound you magnify.

**Maraytaii, I resonate
with song that opens cosmic gate.
Your melody makes me vibrate
my sense of self I recreate.**

4. I know the purpose of this world
is Christ within me to unfurl.
In midst of life's infernal din,
a victory for Christ I win.

O Cosmic Mother, I now hear,
the subtle sound of Sacred Sphere.
As I attune to Cosmic Hum,
the lesser self I overcome.

Maraytaii, I resonate
with song that opens cosmic gate.
Your melody makes me vibrate
my sense of self I recreate.

5. I know surrender is the key,
to self-transcending alchemy.
The thought that problems I must solve,
this is the chain that I dissolve.

O Cosmic Mother, take me home,
I am in sync with Sacred OM,
The sound of sounds will raise me up,
so only light is in my cup.

Maraytaii, I resonate
with song that opens cosmic gate.
Your melody makes me vibrate
my sense of self I recreate.

6. To outer mind it seems so strange,
but there is nothing I must change.
Behind appearances unreal,
I only need the Christ reveal.

O Cosmic Mother, I will be,
a part of cosmic symphony.
All that I AM, an instrument,
for sound that is from heaven sent.

**Maraytaii, I resonate
with song that opens cosmic gate.
Your melody makes me vibrate
my sense of self I recreate.**

7. With Christ illusion I now shatter,
my Spirit is not bound by matter.
The worldly prince we overthrow,
immersed we are in sacred flow.

O Cosmic Mother, I now call,
to enter sacred music hall.
I will be part of life's ascent,
towards the starry firmament.

**Maraytaii, I resonate
with song that opens cosmic gate.
Your melody makes me vibrate
my sense of self I recreate.**

8. No matter what the devil's ploy,
I now accept that life is joy.
And thus with Christ I judge no man,
as I affirm the cosmic plan.

O Cosmic Mother, tune my strings,
my total being with you sings.
Your song I now reverberate,
as cosmic love I celebrate.

**Maraytaii, I resonate
with song that opens cosmic gate.
Your melody makes me vibrate
my sense of self I recreate.**

9. For when I turn the other cheek,
I will join forces with the meek.
And we inherit shall the earth,
the Golden Age is given birth.

O Cosmic Mother, I love you,
your love song keeps me ever true.
You fill me with your sacred tone,
and thus I never feel alone.

**Maraytaii, I resonate
with song that opens cosmic gate.
Your melody makes me vibrate
my sense of self I recreate.**

MA-RAY-TA-II
(Chant 9X, 33X or more)

Sealing

In the name of the Divine Mother, I call to Maraytaii and Mother Mary for the sealing of myself and all people in my circle of influence in the creative flow of the Divine Mother, the River of Life. I call for the multiplication of my calls by all representatives of the Divine Mother, so that we form the perfect figure-eight flow of "As Above, so below." Thus, I accept that this is fully manifest, because the mouth of the Lord, the Divine Mother that I AM, has spoken it. Amen.

DECREE TO MARAYTAII

In the name I AM THAT I AM, Jesus Christ, I call to all representatives of the Divine Mother, especially Maraytaii and Mother Mary, for the healing of my four lower bodies, especially for the transfiguration of my identity body, my sense of self. I call forth the transcendence of all illusions of a separate self, including...

[Make personal calls.]

> 1. O Cosmic Mother, sound the gong,
> that calls me home where I belong.
> I know you love me tenderly,
> and in that knowing I am free.
>
> **Maraytaii, I resonate**
> **with song that opens cosmic gate.**
> **Your melody makes me vibrate**
> **my sense of self I recreate.**
>
> 2. O Cosmic Mother, hold me tight,
> I resonate with your own light.
> Your music purifies my heart,
> your love to all I do impart.

**Maraytaii, I resonate
with song that opens cosmic gate.
Your melody makes me vibrate
my sense of self I recreate.**

3. O Cosmic Mother, we are one,
your heart is like a blazing sun.
My being can but amplify,
the sacred sound you magnify.

**Maraytaii, I resonate
with song that opens cosmic gate.
Your melody makes me vibrate
my sense of self I recreate.**

4. O Cosmic Mother, I now hear,
the subtle sound of Sacred Sphere.
As I attune to Cosmic Hum,
the lesser self I overcome.

**Maraytaii, I resonate
with song that opens cosmic gate.
Your melody makes me vibrate
my sense of self I recreate.**

5. O Cosmic Mother, take me home,
I am in sync with Sacred OM,
The sound of sounds will raise me up,
so only light is in my cup.

**Maraytaii, I resonate
with song that opens cosmic gate.
Your melody makes me vibrate
my sense of self I recreate.**

6. O Cosmic Mother, I will be,
a part of cosmic symphony.
All that I AM, an instrument,
for sound that is from heaven sent.

**Maraytaii, I resonate
with song that opens cosmic gate.
Your melody makes me vibrate
my sense of self I recreate.**

7. O Cosmic Mother, I now call,
to enter sacred music hall.
I will be part of life's ascent,
towards the starry firmament.

**Maraytaii, I resonate
with song that opens cosmic gate.
Your melody makes me vibrate
my sense of self I recreate.**

8. O Cosmic Mother, tune my strings,
my total being with you sings.
Your song I now reverberate,
as cosmic love I celebrate.

Maraytaii, I resonate
with song that opens cosmic gate.
Your melody makes me vibrate
my sense of self I recreate.

9. O Cosmic Mother, I love you,
your love song keeps me ever true.
You fill me with your sacred tone,
and thus I never feel alone.

Maraytaii, I resonate
with song that opens cosmic gate.
Your melody makes me vibrate
my sense of self I recreate.

Sealing

In the name of the Divine Mother, I call to Maraytaii and Mother Mary for the sealing of myself and all people in my circle of influence in the creative flow of the Divine Mother, the River of Life. I call for the multiplication of my calls by all representatives of the Divine Mother, so that we form the perfect figure-eight flow of "As Above, so below." Thus, I accept that this is fully manifest, because the mouth of the Lord, the Divine Mother that I AM, has spoken it. Amen.

Song of Life 2

A NEW MIND

In the name I AM THAT I AM, Jesus Christ, I call to all representatives of the Divine Mother, especially Nada and Mother Mary, for the healing of my four lower bodies, especially for the transfiguration of my mental body. I call forth my freedom from all dualistic illusions, including…

[Make personal calls.]

> When Father-Mother are as One,
> I see the rising of the Son.
> My Christic balance is the key,
> extremes they cannot capture me.
>
> When I am centered in the One,
> my inner balance I have won.
> My I AM Presence now can do,
> all that it wants through Conscious You.
>
> When I have balanced Yang and Yin,
> the victory of Christ I win.
> As Mara's demons I transcend,
> the eightfold path I do ascend.

When I complete the sacred quest,
fulfilling every subtle test.
With Jesus I the ghost release,
Gautama Buddha shows me peace.

When with Maitreya I am free,
Sanat Kumara greeting me.
Alpha-Omega are now one,
I am with them in Central Sun.

When nexus of their figure-eight,
opens up the cosmic gate.
With my Creator I can be,
I AM in true polarity.

When I return to planet earth,
a brand new Self is given birth.
I know now what for all is best,
the Will of God is manifest.

1. There is no separate mind

1. The Noble Truth I seek to find,
and that truth is that all is mind.
If I want to transcend my role,
unruly mind I must control.

O Nada, blessed cosmic grace,
filling up my inner space.
Your song is like a sacred balm,
my mind a sea of perfect calm.

With Nada's secret melody,
my mind remains forever free.
Conducting Nada's symphony,
eternal peace I do decree.

2. Yet mind control involves a twist,
for separate mind does not exist.
There is no separate mind to find,
the concept must be left behind.

O Nada, in your Buddhic mind,
my inner peace I truly find.
As I your song reverberate,
your love I do assimilate.

With Nada's secret melody,
my mind remains forever free.
Conducting Nada's symphony,
eternal peace I do decree.

3. The mind that thinks it is apart,
is out of greater mind a part.
As I absorb this sacred fact,
as separate self I won't react.

O Nada, beauty so sublime,
I follow you beyond all time.
In soundless sound we do immerse,
to recreate the universe.

With Nada's secret melody,
my mind remains forever free.
Conducting Nada's symphony,
eternal peace I do decree.

4. Obscurity or world-wide fame,
I see it all as ego game.
For seeking separate self to raise,
will never win me masters' praise.

O Nada, future we predict
where nothing Christhood can restrict.
With Buddhic mind we do perceive,
a better future we conceive.

With Nada's secret melody,
my mind remains forever free.
Conducting Nada's symphony,
eternal peace I do decree.

5. I seek to be the open door,
nothing less and nothing more.
My I AM Presence I let do,
my mind is one; no longer two.

O Nada, future we rewrite,
where might is never, ever right.
Instead, the mind of Christ is king,
we see the Christ in every thing.

With Nada's secret melody,
my mind remains forever free.
Conducting Nada's symphony,
eternal peace I do decree.

6. On Middle Way I aim to be,
my mind beyond duality.
I see through Mara's ancient scheme,
avoiding this or that extreme.

O Nada, peace is now the norm,
my Spirit is beyond all form.
To form I will no more adapt,
I use potential yet untapped.

With Nada's secret melody,
my mind remains forever free.
Conducting Nada's symphony,
eternal peace I do decree.

7. My separate self I now let go,
I am the Presence here below.
I see now with the single eye,
exposing the satanic lie.

O Nada, such resplendent joy,
my life I truly can enjoy.
I am allowed to have some fun,
my solar plexus like a sun.

With Nada's secret melody,
my mind remains forever free.
Conducting Nada's symphony,
eternal peace I do decree.

8. In River of Life I ever flow,
as God's extension here below.
From oneness I will not depart,
of Buddhic Mind I am a part.

O Nada, service is the key,
to living in reality.
For I see now that life is one,
my highest service has begun.

With Nada's secret melody,
my mind remains forever free.
Conducting Nada's symphony,
eternal peace I do decree.

9. From lies that spring from separate me,
the Buddhic mind now sets me free.
In Mother's love and Father's will,
the Christ does raise me higher still.

O Nada, we do now decree,
that life on earth shall be carefree.
With Jesus we complete the quest,
God's kingdom is now manifest.

**With Nada's secret melody,
my mind remains forever free.
Conducting Nada's symphony,
eternal peace I do decree.**

2. Transcending the epic struggle

1. The mind for'er wants me to feel,
that with its problems I must deal.
The mind creates a special spin,
that epic battle I must win.

O Nada, blessed cosmic grace,
filling up my inner space.
Your song is like a sacred balm,
my mind a sea of perfect calm.

**With Nada's secret melody,
my mind remains forever free.
Conducting Nada's symphony,
eternal peace I do decree.**

2. A mind that is a system closed,
to mortal error is disposed.
It aims for immortality,
through serpentine duality.

O Nada, in your Buddhic mind,
my inner peace I truly find.
As I your song reverberate,
your love I do assimilate.

With Nada's secret melody,
my mind remains forever free.
Conducting Nada's symphony,
eternal peace I do decree.

3. For opposites are always linked,
and thus if one became extinct,
the other one would cease to be,
and thus there is no victory.

O Nada, beauty so sublime,
I follow you beyond all time.
In soundless sound we do immerse,
to recreate the universe.

With Nada's secret melody,
my mind remains forever free.
Conducting Nada's symphony,
eternal peace I do decree.

4. This epic struggle will not end,
until the mindset I transcend.
And thus, I simply walk away,
refusing ego games to play.

O Nada, future we predict
where nothing Christhood can restrict.
With Buddhic mind we do perceive,
a better future we conceive.

With Nada's secret melody,
my mind remains forever free.
Conducting Nada's symphony,
eternal peace I do decree.

5. When I no problem seek to solve,
the separate self I can dissolve.
And as I give up separateness,
in oneness I find true success.

O Nada, future we rewrite,
where might is never, ever right.
Instead, the mind of Christ is king,
we see the Christ in every thing.

With Nada's secret melody,
my mind remains forever free.
Conducting Nada's symphony,
eternal peace I do decree.

6. The separate mind seeks to define,
a self that's based on "me" and "mine."
When ownership I do let go,
I see that mind is truly flow.

O Nada, peace is now the norm,
my Spirit is beyond all form.
To form I will no more adapt,
I use potential yet untapped.

With Nada's secret melody,
my mind remains forever free.
Conducting Nada's symphony,
eternal peace I do decree.

7. And thus I give up futile quest,
to find a self that is at rest.
I see that mind is never still,
but flowing with creative will.

O Nada, such resplendent joy,
my life I truly can enjoy.
I am allowed to have some fun,
my solar plexus like a sun.

With Nada's secret melody,
my mind remains forever free.
Conducting Nada's symphony,
eternal peace I do decree.

8. The only way to mind perfect,
is to attention redirect.
And when my focus I command,
the mind no longer like quicksand.

O Nada, service is the key,
to living in reality.
For I see now that life is one,
my highest service has begun.

With Nada's secret melody,
my mind remains forever free.
Conducting Nada's symphony,
eternal peace I do decree.

9. When I no longer seek to hold,
the mind within a little fold,
I go beyond rigidity,
to unbound creativity.

O Nada, we do now decree,
that life on earth shall be carefree.
With Jesus we complete the quest,
God's kingdom is now manifest.

With Nada's secret melody,
my mind remains forever free.
Conducting Nada's symphony,
eternal peace I do decree.

3. Reborn is my mind

1. The mind is a conglomerate,
my future seeking to dictate.
The ego says the die is cast,
by choices made in distant past.

O Nada, blessed cosmic grace,
filling up my inner space.
Your song is like a sacred balm,
my mind a sea of perfect calm.

With Nada's secret melody,
my mind remains forever free.
Conducting Nada's symphony,
eternal peace I do decree.

2. Yet even karma's strongest mold,
my pure awareness cannot hold.
For I can choose to think anew,
my mind is fresh as morning dew.

O Nada, in your Buddhic mind,
my inner peace I truly find.
As I your song reverberate,
your love I do assimilate.

With Nada's secret melody,
my mind remains forever free.
Conducting Nada's symphony,
eternal peace I do decree.

3. And when I see with childlike mind,
my innocence I surely find.
And now I leave behind the past,
and open up a future vast.

O Nada, beauty so sublime,
I follow you beyond all time.
In soundless sound we do immerse,
to recreate the universe.

With Nada's secret melody,
my mind remains forever free.
Conducting Nada's symphony,
eternal peace I do decree.

4. And as my mind is free to roam,
it seeks to find its starry home.
My thoughts no longer from below,
but what my Presence does bestow.

O Nada, future we predict
where nothing Christhood can restrict.
With Buddhic mind we do perceive,
a better future we conceive.

With Nada's secret melody,
my mind remains forever free.
Conducting Nada's symphony,
eternal peace I do decree.

5. For what is there to figure out,
when Presence knows beyond a doubt,
what is the better thing to do,
so to my Presence I AM true.

O Nada, future we rewrite,
where might is never, ever right.
Instead, the mind of Christ is king,
we see the Christ in every thing.

With Nada's secret melody,
my mind remains forever free.
Conducting Nada's symphony,
eternal peace I do decree.

6. I have no need to analyze,
with intellect that is so wise.
I have no need for asking "why,"
for what is there to justify?

O Nada, peace is now the norm,
my Spirit is beyond all form.
To form I will no more adapt,
I use potential yet untapped.

With Nada's secret melody,
my mind remains forever free.
Conducting Nada's symphony,
eternal peace I do decree.

7. I set my mind on better course,
that leads me back towards my source.
All lesser thoughts I just let go,
surrendering to sacred flow.

O Nada, such resplendent joy,
my life I truly can enjoy.
I am allowed to have some fun,
my solar plexus like a sun.

With Nada's secret melody,
my mind remains forever free.
Conducting Nada's symphony,
eternal peace I do decree.

8. And now my mind is truly freed,
sophistication I don't need.
The serpent now has naught in me,
for I want only to be free.

O Nada, service is the key,
to living in reality.
For I see now that life is one,
my highest service has begun.

With Nada's secret melody,
my mind remains forever free.
Conducting Nada's symphony,
eternal peace I do decree.

9. To Eden I have now returned,
my lessons well and truly learned.
In oneness with Maitreya's mind,
I master every shade of "kind."

O Nada, we do now decree,
that life on earth shall be carefree.
With Jesus we complete the quest,
God's kingdom is now manifest.

With Nada's secret melody,
my mind remains forever free.
Conducting Nada's symphony,
eternal peace I do decree.

4. Reclaiming my innocence

1. Awakening to innocence,
gives me a better inner sense.
The truth is now so crystal clear,
the mind creates the matter sphere.

O Nada, blessed cosmic grace,
filling up my inner space.
Your song is like a sacred balm,
my mind a sea of perfect calm.

With Nada's secret melody,
my mind remains forever free.
Conducting Nada's symphony,
eternal peace I do decree.

2. I see that mind is one great whole,
I seek to raise collective soul.
There is no room for "me" and "mine,"
a whole new world I do define.

O Nada, in your Buddhic mind,
my inner peace I truly find.
As I your song reverberate,
your love I do assimilate.

**With Nada's secret melody,
my mind remains forever free.
Conducting Nada's symphony,
eternal peace I do decree.**

3. All judgment I now rise above,
I see through eyes of purest love.
I shatter lies of "good and bad,"
designed to drive all people mad.

O Nada, beauty so sublime,
I follow you beyond all time.
In soundless sound we do immerse,
to recreate the universe.

**With Nada's secret melody,
my mind remains forever free.
Conducting Nada's symphony,
eternal peace I do decree.**

4. Divide and conquer is the ploy,
of those who only can destroy.
Yet if we turn the other cheek,
the earth is given to the meek.

O Nada, future we predict
where nothing Christhood can restrict.
With Buddhic mind we do perceive,
a better future we conceive.

**With Nada's secret melody,
my mind remains forever free.
Conducting Nada's symphony,
eternal peace I do decree.**

5. With Christ I now extend a hand,
to those still part of devil's band.
For those who cosmic love reject,
Christ's judgment will be the effect.

O Nada, future we rewrite,
where might is never, ever right.
Instead, the mind of Christ is king,
we see the Christ in every thing.

**With Nada's secret melody,
my mind remains forever free.
Conducting Nada's symphony,
eternal peace I do decree.**

6. I take my stand on Christic rock,
unmoved by those who seek to mock.
As they are taken from the earth,
a golden age is given birth.

O Nada, peace is now the norm,
my Spirit is beyond all form.
To form I will no more adapt,
I use potential yet untapped.

**With Nada's secret melody,
my mind remains forever free.
Conducting Nada's symphony,
eternal peace I do decree.**

7. All those who oneness will embrace,
of one accord find cosmic grace.
Our minds now form a giant wave,
to raise the earth beyond the grave.

O Nada, such resplendent joy,
my life I truly can enjoy.
I am allowed to have some fun,
my solar plexus like a sun.

**With Nada's secret melody,
my mind remains forever free.
Conducting Nada's symphony,
eternal peace I do decree.**

8. A future oneness I now see,
from separation all are free.
As we reject the devil's game,
our innocence we do reclaim.

O Nada, service is the key,
to living in reality.
For I see now that life is one,
my highest service has begun.

With Nada's secret melody,
my mind remains forever free.
Conducting Nada's symphony,
eternal peace I do decree.

9. And Mother Earth now shows a smile,
as nowhere seen for quite a while.
Her children are set free to play,
as we embrace a brand new day.

O Nada, we do now decree,
that life on earth shall be carefree.
With Jesus we complete the quest,
God's kingdom is now manifest.

With Nada's secret melody,
my mind remains forever free.
Conducting Nada's symphony,
eternal peace I do decree.

OM AH HUM,
NADA GURU PADME SIDDHI HUM

(Chant 9X, 33X or more)

Sealing

In the name of the Divine Mother, I call to Nada and Mother Mary for the sealing of myself and all people in my circle of influence in the creative flow of the Divine Mother, the River of Life. I call for the multiplication of my calls by all representatives of the Divine Mother, so that we form the perfect figure-eight flow of "As Above, so below." Thus, I accept that this is fully manifest, because the mouth of the Lord, the Divine Mother that I AM, has spoken it. Amen.

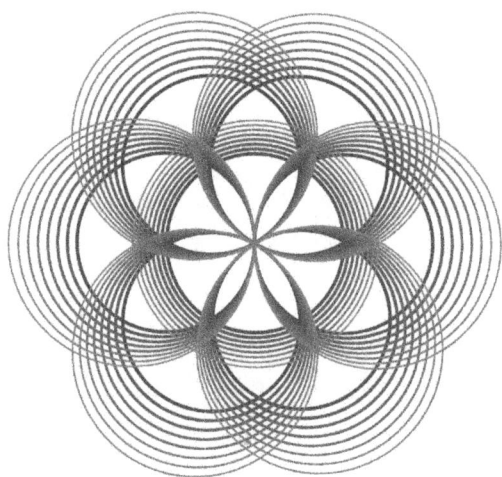

DECREE TO NADA

In the name I AM THAT I AM, Jesus Christ, I call to all representatives of the Divine Mother, especially Nada and Mother Mary, for the healing of my four lower bodies, especially for the transfiguration of my mental body. I call forth my freedom from all dualistic illusions, including...

[Make personal calls.]

1. O Nada, blessed cosmic grace,
filling up my inner space.
Your song is like a sacred balm,
my mind a sea of perfect calm.

**With Nada's secret melody,
my mind remains forever free.
Conducting Nada's symphony,
eternal peace I do decree.**

2. O Nada, in your Buddhic mind,
my inner peace I truly find.
As I your song reverberate,
your love I do assimilate.

**With Nada's secret melody,
my mind remains forever free.
Conducting Nada's symphony,
eternal peace I do decree.**

3. O Nada, beauty so sublime,
I follow you beyond all time.
In soundless sound we do immerse,
to recreate the universe.

**With Nada's secret melody,
my mind remains forever free.
Conducting Nada's symphony,
eternal peace I do decree.**

4. O Nada, future we predict
where nothing Christhood can restrict.
With Buddhic mind we do perceive,
a better future we conceive.

**With Nada's secret melody,
my mind remains forever free.
Conducting Nada's symphony,
eternal peace I do decree.**

5. O Nada, future we rewrite,
where might is never, ever right.
Instead, the mind of Christ is king,
we see the Christ in every thing.

With Nada's secret melody,
my mind remains forever free.
Conducting Nada's symphony,
eternal peace I do decree.

6. O Nada, peace is now the norm,
my Spirit is beyond all form.
To form I will no more adapt,
I use potential yet untapped.

With Nada's secret melody,
my mind remains forever free.
Conducting Nada's symphony,
eternal peace I do decree.

7. O Nada, such resplendent joy,
my life I truly can enjoy.
I am allowed to have some fun,
my solar plexus like a sun.

With Nada's secret melody,
my mind remains forever free.
Conducting Nada's symphony,
eternal peace I do decree.

8. O Nada, service is the key,
to living in reality.
For I see now that life is one,
my highest service has begun.

**With Nada's secret melody,
my mind remains forever free.
Conducting Nada's symphony,
eternal peace I do decree.**

9. O Nada, we do now decree,
that life on earth shall be carefree.
With Jesus we complete the quest,
God's kingdom is now manifest.

**With Nada's secret melody,
my mind remains forever free.
Conducting Nada's symphony,
eternal peace I do decree.**

Sealing

In the name of the Divine Mother, I call to Nada and Mother Mary for the sealing of myself and all people in my circle of influence in the creative flow of the Divine Mother, the River of Life. I call for the multiplication of my calls by all representatives of the Divine Mother, so that we form the perfect figure-eight flow of "As Above, so below." Thus, I accept that this is fully manifest, because the mouth of the Lord, the Divine Mother that I AM, has spoken it. Amen.

Song of Life 3

A New Emotional Body

In the name I AM THAT I AM, Jesus Christ, I call to all representatives of the Divine Mother, especially Kuan Yin and Mother Mary, for the healing of my four lower bodies, especially for the transfiguration of my emotional body and my feelings. I call forth the healing of all emotional wounds, including...

[Make personal calls.]

> When Father-Mother are as One,
> I see the rising of the Son.
> My Christic balance is the key,
> extremes they cannot capture me.
>
> When I am centered in the One,
> my inner balance I have won.
> My I AM Presence now can do,
> all that it wants through Conscious You.
>
> When I have balanced Yang and Yin,
> the victory of Christ I win.
> As Mara's demons I transcend,
> the eightfold path I do ascend.

When I complete the sacred quest,
fulfilling every subtle test.
With Jesus I the ghost release,
Gautama Buddha shows me peace.

When with Maitreya I am free,
Sanat Kumara greeting me.
Alpha-Omega are now one,
I am with them in Central Sun.

When nexus of their figure-eight,
opens up the cosmic gate.
With my Creator I can be,
I AM in true polarity.

When I return to planet earth,
a brand new Self is given birth.
I know now what for all is best,
the Will of God is manifest.

1. From fear to love

1. O Song of Life, sound so sublime,
you shatter veil of space and time.
I see that feelings are the key
to releasing creativity.

O Kuan Yin, what sacred name,
fill me now with Mercy's Flame.
In giving mercy I am free,
forgiving all is magic key.

In Kuan Yin's sweet melody,
I am set free my Self to be.
In Kuan Yin's vitality,
I claim my immortality.

2. My heart beats one with sacred chime,
as I transcend old paradigm.
For as I see a new precept,
my feeling body I accept.

O Kuan Yin, I now let go,
of all attachments here below.
All pent-up feelings I release,
free from emotional disease.

In Kuan Yin's sweet melody,
I am set free my Self to be.
In Kuan Yin's vitality,
I claim my immortality.

3. As I now grasp a higher goal,
my feelings I need not control.
For feelings are just energy,
with instant alterability.

O Kuan Yin, why must I feel,
that life falls short of my ideal?
All expectations I give up,
my mind is now an empty cup

In Kuan Yin's sweet melody,
I am set free my Self to be.
In Kuan Yin's vitality,
I claim my immortality.

4. The devil's oh so subtle ploy
is that my feelings I destroy.
Instead I now accelerate
all feelings to a higher state.

O Kuan Yin, transcend the past,
as all resentment gone at last.
From future nothing I expect,
eternal now I won't reject.

In Kuan Yin's sweet melody,
I am set free my Self to be.
In Kuan Yin's vitality,
I claim my immortality.

5. I use my mind's ability
to alter feeling energy.
Ascended masters I invite
as I invoke the sacred light.

O Kuan Yin, uplifting me,
beyond Samsara's raging sea.
All safe inside your Prajna boat,
the farther shore no more remote.

In Kuan Yin's sweet melody,
I am set free my Self to be.
In Kuan Yin's vitality,
I claim my immortality.

6. The light my feelings will transform,
as peace is now the brand new norm.
The masters give me reference
for feeling God's magnificence.

O Kuan Yin, your alchemy,
with miracles you set me free.
As I forgive, I am forgiven,
by guilt I am no longer driven.

In Kuan Yin's sweet melody,
I am set free my Self to be.
In Kuan Yin's vitality,
I claim my immortality.

7. Beyond conditions is the love,
that rains upon me from above.
And this becomes the standard I
all feelings now am judging by.

O Kuan Yin, all worries gone,
with nothing done, no thing undone.
Through separate self I will not do,
and thus I rest, all one with you.

In Kuan Yin's sweet melody,
I am set free my Self to be.
In Kuan Yin's vitality,
I claim my immortality.

8. For when I feel the masters near,
I know that love replaces fear.
I know that when I do my part,
all fear is banished from my heart.

O Kuan Yin, your sanity,
now sets me free from vanity.
For truly, what is that to me;
I just let go and follow thee.

In Kuan Yin's sweet melody,
I am set free my Self to be.
In Kuan Yin's vitality,
I claim my immortality.

9. As my conditions I release,
my feeling body is at peace.
I now surrender to my Source,
and thus I plot a brand new course.

O Kuan Yin, so sweet the sound,
that emanates from holy ground.
As I let go of ego's chore,
I find myself on farther shore.

In Kuan Yin's sweet melody,
I am set free my Self to be.
In Kuan Yin's vitality,
I claim my immortality.

2. I let my feelings flow

1. My feelings are just energy,
and thus I seek the synergy.
With Song of Life I do vibrate,
my feelings ever resonate.

O Kuan Yin, what sacred name,
fill me now with Mercy's Flame.
In giving mercy I am free,
forgiving all is magic key.

In Kuan Yin's sweet melody,
I am set free my Self to be.
In Kuan Yin's vitality,
I claim my immortality.

2. As I hold true to what is dear,
my feelings raised beyond all fear.
All fear transformed by sacred love,
my heart takes flight like holy dove.

O Kuan Yin, I now let go,
of all attachments here below.
All pent-up feelings I release,
free from emotional disease.

In Kuan Yin's sweet melody,
I am set free my Self to be.
In Kuan Yin's vitality,
I claim my immortality.

3. Unending aggressivity
is ego's great proclivity.
Yet I refuse to play along,
for I am filled with life's own song.

O Kuan Yin, why must I feel,
that life falls short of my ideal?
All expectations I give up,
my mind is now an empty cup

In Kuan Yin's sweet melody,
I am set free my Self to be.
In Kuan Yin's vitality,
I claim my immortality.

4. As all resentment I let go,
my feelings freely start to flow,
and with my feelings no more blocked,
my healing truly is unlocked.

O Kuan Yin, transcend the past,
as all resentment gone at last.
From future nothing I expect,
eternal now I won't reject.

In Kuan Yin's sweet melody,
I am set free my Self to be.
In Kuan Yin's vitality,
I claim my immortality.

5. Released from former stress and strife,
my feeling body has new life.
As hardened feelings start to melt,
this is the best I've ever felt.

O Kuan Yin, uplifting me,
beyond Samsara's raging sea.
All safe inside your Prajna boat,
the farther shore no more remote.

In Kuan Yin's sweet melody,
I am set free my Self to be.
In Kuan Yin's vitality,
I claim my immortality.

6. A ray of sun breaks through the cloud,
I want to rise and sing aloud.
I feel the flow of bubbling joy,
a whole new life I can enjoy.

O Kuan Yin, your alchemy,
with miracles you set me free.
As I forgive, I am forgiven,
by guilt I am no longer driven.

In Kuan Yin's sweet melody,
I am set free my Self to be.
In Kuan Yin's vitality,
I claim my immortality.

7. In basement of subconscious mind,
no hardened feelings left behind.
The Holy Spirit clears the room,
from sense of an impending doom.

O Kuan Yin, all worries gone,
with nothing done, no thing undone.
Through separate self I will not do,
and thus I rest, all one with you.

In Kuan Yin's sweet melody,
I am set free my Self to be.
In Kuan Yin's vitality,
I claim my immortality.

8. The old chaotic energy,
is now replaced by harmony.
And in this newly hallowed space,
begins to grow a sense of grace.

O Kuan Yin, your sanity,
now sets me free from vanity.
For truly, what is that to me;
I just let go and follow thee.

In Kuan Yin's sweet melody,
I am set free my Self to be.
In Kuan Yin's vitality,
I claim my immortality.

9. As I let go of former ties,
deep gratitude begins to rise.
And as the veil begins to lift,
I see that life is such a gift.

O Kuan Yin, so sweet the sound,
that emanates from holy ground.
As I let go of ego's chore,
I find myself on farther shore.

In Kuan Yin's sweet melody,
I am set free my Self to be.
In Kuan Yin's vitality,
I claim my immortality.

3. I master my feelings

1. For self-awareness I give praise,
my sense of self I hereby raise.
A brand new me is given birth,
all filled with joy and childlike mirth.

O Kuan Yin, what sacred name,
fill me now with Mercy's Flame.
In giving mercy I am free,
forgiving all is magic key.

In Kuan Yin's sweet melody,
I am set free my Self to be.
In Kuan Yin's vitality,
I claim my immortality.

2. Some feelings I need not refine,
for lower feelings were not mine.
They came from spirits every one,
and all these spirits now be gone.

O Kuan Yin, I now let go,
of all attachments here below.
All pent-up feelings I release,
free from emotional disease.

In Kuan Yin's sweet melody,
I am set free my Self to be.
In Kuan Yin's vitality,
I claim my immortality.

3. I am the master of my house,
this is the cause I do espouse.
I know that it is not too late,
a former choice to uncreate.

O Kuan Yin, why must I feel,
that life falls short of my ideal?
All expectations I give up,
my mind is now an empty cup

In Kuan Yin's sweet melody,
I am set free my Self to be.
In Kuan Yin's vitality,
I claim my immortality.

4. As I take back my force of will,
I feel that life is such a thrill.
As I now make a Christic choice,
in newfound freedom I rejoice.

O Kuan Yin, transcend the past,
as all resentment gone at last.
From future nothing I expect,
eternal now I won't reject.

In Kuan Yin's sweet melody,
I am set free my Self to be.
In Kuan Yin's vitality,
I claim my immortality.

5. Aggressive spirits now must clear,
you are no longer wanted here.
Instead I now bid enter in,
my blessed master, Kuan Yin.

O Kuan Yin, uplifting me,
beyond Samsara's raging sea.
All safe inside your Prajna boat,
the farther shore no more remote.

In Kuan Yin's sweet melody,
I am set free my Self to be.
In Kuan Yin's vitality,
I claim my immortality.

6. With you so near, how can I fret,
I now surrender and forget.
And thus you carry me along,
on wings of most enchanting song.

O Kuan Yin, your alchemy,
with miracles you set me free.
As I forgive, I am forgiven,
by guilt I am no longer driven.

In Kuan Yin's sweet melody,
I am set free my Self to be.
In Kuan Yin's vitality,
I claim my immortality.

7. I enter now your Prajna boat,
enthralled by sound of your keynote.
As grudges all I leave behind,
in rays of dawn no longer blind.

O Kuan Yin, all worries gone,
with nothing done, no thing undone.
Through separate self I will not do,
and thus I rest, all one with you.

In Kuan Yin's sweet melody,
I am set free my Self to be.
In Kuan Yin's vitality,
I claim my immortality.

8. No spirit can me agitate,
Samsara's Sea we navigate.
My heart lets out a lion's roar,
as I catch glimpse of farther shore.

O Kuan Yin, your sanity,
now sets me free from vanity.
For truly, what is that to me;
I just let go and follow thee.

In Kuan Yin's sweet melody,
I am set free my Self to be.
In Kuan Yin's vitality,
I claim my immortality.

9. O Kuan, Yin, my faith in you,
Mara's demons I pass through.
For all the world I would not miss,
my entrance into Buddhic Bliss.

O Kuan Yin, so sweet the sound,
that emanates from holy ground.
As I let go of ego's chore,
I find myself on farther shore.

In Kuan Yin's sweet melody,
I am set free my Self to be.
In Kuan Yin's vitality,
I claim my immortality.

4. My feelings play a symphony

1. This newfound bliss of feeling world,
into my body I unfurl.
It penetrates through every cell,
clearing them from curse of hell.

O Kuan Yin, what sacred name,
fill me now with Mercy's Flame.
In giving mercy I am free,
forgiving all is magic key.

In Kuan Yin's sweet melody,
I am set free my Self to be.
In Kuan Yin's vitality,
I claim my immortality.

2. My feelings are the instrument,
for music from my Presence sent.
My I AM Presence in command,
I play my part in master's band.

O Kuan Yin, I now let go,
of all attachments here below.
All pent-up feelings I release,
free from emotional disease.

In Kuan Yin's sweet melody,
I am set free my Self to be.
In Kuan Yin's vitality,
I claim my immortality.

3. My feelings play a symphony,
that fills me with vitality.
As they no longer are deprived,
each cell and organ is revived.

O Kuan Yin, why must I feel,
that life falls short of my ideal?
All expectations I give up,
my mind is now an empty cup.

In Kuan Yin's sweet melody,
I am set free my Self to be.
In Kuan Yin's vitality,
I claim my immortality.

4. As sacred symphony performed,
all illness is by sound transformed.
My I AM Presence is my wealth,
it gives my body perfect health.

O Kuan Yin, transcend the past,
as all resentment gone at last.
From future nothing I expect,
eternal now I won't reject.

In Kuan Yin's sweet melody,
I am set free my Self to be.
In Kuan Yin's vitality,
I claim my immortality.

5. My feelings and my body cleared,
my I AM Presence is revered.
My perfect health is manifest,
as I am filled with boundless zest.

O Kuan Yin, uplifting me,
beyond Samsara's raging sea.
All safe inside your Prajna boat,
the farther shore no more remote.

In Kuan Yin's sweet melody,
I am set free my Self to be.
In Kuan Yin's vitality,
I claim my immortality.

6. As instant healing I accept,
I know the promise has been kept.
For Jesus said what'er I ask,
he always is up to the task.

O Kuan Yin, your alchemy,
with miracles you set me free.
As I forgive, I am forgiven,
by guilt I am no longer driven.

In Kuan Yin's sweet melody,
I am set free my Self to be.
In Kuan Yin's vitality,
I claim my immortality.

7. In body mine, Christ is the king,
my cells and atoms with him sing.
With miracle from Kuan Yin,
my perfect health I hereby win.

O Kuan Yin, all worries gone,
with nothing done, no thing undone.
Through separate self I will not do,
and thus I rest, all one with you.

In Kuan Yin's sweet melody,
I am set free my Self to be.
In Kuan Yin's vitality,
I claim my immortality.

8. I feel God's unrelenting power,
each cell unfolding like a flower.
My I AM Presence in control,
my body now a perfect whole.

O Kuan Yin, your sanity,
now sets me free from vanity.
For truly, what is that to me;
I just let go and follow thee.

In Kuan Yin's sweet melody,
I am set free my Self to be.
In Kuan Yin's vitality,
I claim my immortality.

9. My quest for wholeness a success,
and thus all life I truly bless.
As healing rays I radiate,
a better world I co-create.

O Kuan Yin, so sweet the sound,
that emanates from holy ground.
As I let go of ego's chore,
I find myself on farther shore.

In Kuan Yin's sweet melody,
I am set free my Self to be.
In Kuan Yin's vitality,
I claim my immortality.

OM MANI PADME HUM
(Chant 9X, 33X or more)

Sealing

In the name of the Divine Mother, I call to Kuan Yin and Mother Mary for the sealing of myself and all people in my circle of influence in the creative flow of the Divine Mother, the River of Life. I call for the multiplication of my calls by all representatives of the Divine Mother, so that we form the perfect figure-eight flow of "As Above, so below." Thus, I accept that this is fully manifest, because the mouth of the Lord, the Divine Mother that I AM, has spoken it. Amen.

DECREE TO KUAN YIN

In the name I AM THAT I AM, Jesus Christ, I call to all representatives of the Divine Mother, especially Kuan Yin and Mother Mary, for the healing of my four lower bodies, especially for the transfiguration of my emotional body and my feelings. I call forth the healing of all emotional wounds, including...

[Make personal calls.]

1. O Kuan Yin, what sacred name,
fill me now with Mercy's Flame.
In giving mercy I am free,
forgiving all is magic key.

In Kuan Yin's sweet melody,
I am set free my Self to be.
In Kuan Yin's vitality,
I claim my immortality.

2. O Kuan Yin, I now let go,
of all attachments here below.
All pent-up feelings I release,
free from emotional disease.

In Kuan Yin's sweet melody,
I am set free my Self to be.
In Kuan Yin's vitality,
I claim my immortality.

3. O Kuan Yin, why must I feel,
that life falls short of my ideal?
All expectations I give up,
my mind is now an empty cup

In Kuan Yin's sweet melody,
I am set free my Self to be.
In Kuan Yin's vitality,
I claim my immortality.

4. O Kuan Yin, transcend the past,
as all resentment gone at last.
From future nothing I expect,
eternal now I won't reject.

In Kuan Yin's sweet melody,
I am set free my Self to be.
In Kuan Yin's vitality,
I claim my immortality.

5. O Kuan Yin, uplifting me,
beyond Samsara's raging sea.
All safe inside your Prajna boat,
the farther shore no more remote.

In Kuan Yin's sweet melody,
I am set free my Self to be.
In Kuan Yin's vitality,
I claim my immortality.

6. O Kuan Yin, your alchemy,
with miracles you set me free.
As I forgive, I am forgiven,
by guilt I am no longer driven.

In Kuan Yin's sweet melody,
I am set free my Self to be.
In Kuan Yin's vitality,
I claim my immortality.

7. O Kuan Yin, all worries gone,
with nothing done, no thing undone.
Through separate self I will not do,
and thus I rest, all one with you.

In Kuan Yin's sweet melody,
I am set free my Self to be.
In Kuan Yin's vitality,
I claim my immortality.

8. O Kuan Yin, your sanity,
now sets me free from vanity.
For truly, what is that to me;
I just let go and follow thee.

In Kuan Yin's sweet melody,
I am set free my Self to be.
In Kuan Yin's vitality,
I claim my immortality.

9. O Kuan Yin, so sweet the sound,
that emanates from holy ground.
As I let go of ego's chore,
I find myself on farther shore.

**In Kuan Yin's sweet melody,
I am set free my Self to be.
In Kuan Yin's vitality,
I claim my immortality.**

Sealing

In the name of the Divine Mother, I call to Kuan Yin and Mother Mary for the sealing of myself and all people in my circle of influence in the creative flow of the Divine Mother, the River of Life. I call for the multiplication of my calls by all representatives of the Divine Mother, so that we form the perfect figure-eight flow of "As Above, so below." Thus, I accept that this is fully manifest, because the mouth of the Lord, the Divine Mother that I AM, has spoken it. Amen.

Song of Life 4

A NEW BODY

In the name I AM THAT I AM, Jesus Christ, I call to all representatives of the Divine Mother, especially Mother Mary, for the healing of my four lower bodies, especially for the transfiguration of my physical body. I call for the healing of all imbalances and diseases, including...

[Make personal calls.]

When Father-Mother are as One,
I see the rising of the Son.
My Christic balance is the key,
extremes they cannot capture me.

When I am centered in the One,
my inner balance I have won.
My I AM Presence now can do,
all that it wants through Conscious You.

When I have balanced Yang and Yin,
the victory of Christ I win.
As Mara's demons I transcend,
the eightfold path I do ascend.

When I complete the sacred quest,
fulfilling every subtle test.
With Jesus I the ghost release,
Gautama Buddha shows me peace.

When with Maitreya I am free,
Sanat Kumara greeting me.
Alpha-Omega are now one,
I am with them in Central Sun.

When nexus of their figure-eight,
opens up the cosmic gate.
With my Creator I can be,
I AM in true polarity.

When I return to planet earth,
a brand new Self is given birth.
I know now what for all is best,
the Will of God is manifest.

1. I claim instant healing

1. My body is but a mirage,
solidity all camouflage.
Projections from four lower minds
is what my body's health defines.

O Blessed Mary's Song of Life,
consuming every form of strife.
As I attune to sound so fair,
each cell is healthy, I declare.

O Mother Mary, generate,
the song that does accelerate,
my cells into a higher state,
in perfect health they scintillate.

2. At one with Christ I do decree,
my body will change instantly.
The perfect image I command,
downloaded to pineal gland.

As life's own song I ever hear,
it does consume all sense of fear.
In tune with Mother's symphony,
from all diseases I AM free.

O Mother Mary, generate,
the song that does accelerate,
my cells into a higher state,
in perfect health they scintillate.

3. I now command my inner eye,
to Christic image magnify.
And then upon all flesh project,
my every cell it will perfect.

In Mother's love I do transcend,
and all my struggles hereby end.
For when with Mother's eye I see,
no imperfection touches me.

O Mother Mary, generate,
the song that does accelerate,
my cells into a higher state,
in perfect health they scintillate.

4. In body's center of Christ mind,
the wheels of aging I rewind.
As all my cells hereby vibrate,
in sync with higher Christic rate.

I see that healing must begin
by finding Living Christ within.
For as I see with single eye,
each cell the light does amplify.

O Mother Mary, generate,
the song that does accelerate,
my cells into a higher state,
in perfect health they scintillate.

5. Eternal youth no fantasy,
I hereby claim my liberty.
This body mine no longer old,
for youthful pattern I unfold.

In Mother's music I am free,
from memories of a lesser me.
My vision in a perfect state,
that all my cells regenerate.

O Mother Mary, generate,
the song that does accelerate,
my cells into a higher state,
in perfect health they scintillate.

6. And now my body spirits four
are burdened by the past no more.
The lie of aging I reject,
life's elixir all cells perfect.

O Mother's Love, sweet melody,
from imperfections I AM free.
O Mother Mary, sound of sounds,
within my heart your love abounds.

O Mother Mary, generate,
the song that does accelerate,
my cells into a higher state,
in perfect health they scintillate.

7. I see that Christ's essential truth,
is fountain of eternal youth.
In life's own waters I submerge,
a younger me I do emerge.

Through Mother's beauty so sublime,
transcending bounds of space and time.
All cells beyond the mortal tomb,
as they are whole in Mother's womb.

O Mother Mary, generate,
the song that does accelerate,
my cells into a higher state,
in perfect health they scintillate.

8. O Death, where is thy fatal sting,
my body spirits all do sing,
along with life's own melody,
I claim my immortality.

In resonance with life's own song,
in life's harmonics I belong.
The blueprint of my perfect state
does every cell reconsecrate.

O Mother Mary, generate,
the song that does accelerate,
my cells into a higher state,
in perfect health they scintillate.

9. O Death, where is your victory,
for Christ does now transfigure me.
My bodies four all filled with light,
I only see with Christic sight.

The tuning fork in every cell
is now attuned to Mother's bell.
From curse of death I AM now free,
I claim my immortality.

O Mother Mary, generate,
the song that does accelerate,
my cells into a higher state,
in perfect health they scintillate.

2. In Mother Mary's loving arms

1. In Mother Mary's loving arms,
I feel reborn to youthful charms.
Her vision I assimilate,
my body does regenerate.

O Blessed Mary's Song of Life,
consuming every form of strife.
As I attune to sound so fair,
each cell is healthy, I declare.

O Mother Mary, generate,
the song that does accelerate,
my cells into a higher state,
in perfect health they scintillate.

2. With Mother Mary I project,
my circulation is perfect.
Immersed in Mother's sacred flow,
my blood emits a sacred glow.

As life's own song I ever hear,
it does consume all sense of fear.
In tune with Mother's symphony,
from all diseases I AM free.

O Mother Mary, generate,
the song that does accelerate,
my cells into a higher state,
in perfect health they scintillate.

3. With Mother Mary I project,
my endocrines are now perfect.
Hormonal harmony I find,
a balanced body, balanced mind.

In Mother's love I do transcend,
and all my struggles hereby end.
For when with Mother's eye I see,
no imperfection touches me.

O Mother Mary, generate,
the song that does accelerate,
my cells into a higher state,
in perfect health they scintillate.

4. With Mother Mary I project,
that my digestion is perfect.
As Mother's nurture I take in,
abundant strength I hereby win.

I see that healing must begin
by finding Living Christ within.
For as I see with single eye,
each cell the light does amplify.

O Mother Mary, generate,
the song that does accelerate,
my cells into a higher state,
in perfect health they scintillate.

5. With Mother Mary I project,
immune defenses are perfect.
My body from all toxins sealed,
my perfect health hereby revealed.

In Mother's music I am free,
from memories of a lesser me.
My vision in a perfect state,
that all my cells regenerate.

O Mother Mary, generate,
the song that does accelerate,
my cells into a higher state,
in perfect health they scintillate.

6. With Mother Mary I project,
Lymphatic system is perfect.
My body fluids circulate,
all tissues in a balanced state.

O Mother's Love, sweet melody,
from imperfections I AM free.
O Mother Mary, sound of sounds,
within my heart your love abounds.

O Mother Mary, generate,
the song that does accelerate,
my cells into a higher state,
in perfect health they scintillate.

7. With Mother Mary I project,
all muscles mine are now perfect.
For every part of me is strong,
I resonate with Mother's song.

Through Mother's beauty so sublime,
transcending bounds of space and time.
All cells beyond the mortal tomb,
as they are whole in Mother's womb.

O Mother Mary, generate,
the song that does accelerate,
my cells into a higher state,
in perfect health they scintillate.

8. With Mother Mary I project,
my nervous system is perfect.
My brain and nerves are in control,
and I am ever on a roll.

In resonance with life's own song,
in life's harmonics I belong.
The blueprint of my perfect state
does every cell reconsecrate.

O Mother Mary, generate,
the song that does accelerate,
my cells into a higher state,
in perfect health they scintillate.

9. With Mother Mary I project,
my reproduction is perfect.
I find my role in the process,
that causes life to e'er progress.

The tuning fork in every cell
is now attuned to Mother's bell.
From curse of death I AM now free,
I claim my immortality.

O Mother Mary, generate,
the song that does accelerate,
my cells into a higher state,
in perfect health they scintillate.

3. My immaculate vision

1. With Mother Mary I project,
my respiration is perfect.
As oxygen brings sacred light,
all toxins instantly take flight.

O Blessed Mary's Song of Life,
consuming every form of strife.
As I attune to sound so fair,
each cell is healthy, I declare.

O Mother Mary, generate,
the song that does accelerate,
my cells into a higher state,
in perfect health they scintillate.

2. With Mother Mary I project,
my bones and marrow are perfect.
The marrow at my very core,
is purer than it was before.

As life's own song I ever hear,
it does consume all sense of fear.
In tune with Mother's symphony,
from all diseases I AM free.

O Mother Mary, generate,
the song that does accelerate,
my cells into a higher state,
in perfect health they scintillate.

3. With Mother Mary I project,
urinaries are perfect.
My body purified of waste,
the perfect health I hereby taste.

In Mother's love I do transcend,
and all my struggles hereby end.
For when with Mother's eye I see,
no imperfection touches me.

O Mother Mary, generate,
the song that does accelerate,
my cells into a higher state,
in perfect health they scintillate.

4. With Mother Mary I project,
my brain and spinal cord perfect.
For Christ is ever in command,
directing all with steady hand.

I see that healing must begin
by finding Living Christ within.
For as I see with single eye,
each cell the light does amplify.

O Mother Mary, generate,
the song that does accelerate,
my cells into a higher state,
in perfect health they scintillate.

5. With Mother Mary I project,
my heart is always most perfect.
With lion's strength I hereby roar,
my heart will beat forevermore.

In Mother's music I am free,
from memories of a lesser me.
My vision in a perfect state,
that all my cells regenerate.

**O Mother Mary, generate,
the song that does accelerate,
my cells into a higher state,
in perfect health they scintillate.**

6. With Mother Mary I project,
my lungs are always most perfect.
The breath of life does me sustain,
my goals in life I do attain.

O Mother's Love, sweet melody,
from imperfections I AM free.
O Mother Mary, sound of sounds,
within my heart your love abounds.

**O Mother Mary, generate,
the song that does accelerate,
my cells into a higher state,
in perfect health they scintillate.**

7. With Mother Mary I project,
my stomach, liver are perfect.
As God's own gifts I do ingest,
the sacred substance I digest.

Through Mother's beauty so sublime,
transcending bounds of space and time.
All cells beyond the mortal tomb,
as they are whole in Mother's womb.

O Mother Mary, generate,
the song that does accelerate,
my cells into a higher state,
in perfect health they scintillate.

8. With Mother Mary I project,
intestines mine are most perfect.
Absorbing only what is best,
they do eliminate the rest.

In resonance with life's own song,
in life's harmonics I belong.
The blueprint of my perfect state
does every cell reconsecrate.

O Mother Mary, generate,
the song that does accelerate,
my cells into a higher state,
in perfect health they scintillate.

9. With Mother Mary I project,
my kidneys always most perfect.
These sacred organs will make sure,
my blood remains forever pure.

The tuning fork in every cell
is now attuned to Mother's bell.
From curse of death I AM now free,
I claim my immortality.

O Mother Mary, generate,
the song that does accelerate,
my cells into a higher state,
in perfect health they scintillate.

4. I claim my healthy body

1. With Mother Mary I project,
my skin is always most perfect.
Absorbing golden light of sun,
a whole new era has begun.

O Blessed Mary's Song of Life,
consuming every form of strife.
As I attune to sound so fair,
each cell is healthy, I declare.

O Mother Mary, generate,
the song that does accelerate,
my cells into a higher state,
in perfect health they scintillate.

2. With Mother Mary I project,
my sexual organs most perfect.
Eliminating all excess,
the force of life I do express.

As life's own song I ever hear,
it does consume all sense of fear.
In tune with Mother's symphony,
from all diseases I AM free.

O Mother Mary, generate,
the song that does accelerate,
my cells into a higher state,
in perfect health they scintillate.

3. With Mother Mary I project,
my body's glands are most perfect.
The hand of Christ does regulate,
the flow that does regenerate.

In Mother's love I do transcend,
and all my struggles hereby end.
For when with Mother's eye I see,
no imperfection touches me.

O Mother Mary, generate,
the song that does accelerate,
my cells into a higher state,
in perfect health they scintillate.

4. My body a united whole,
I am a resurrected soul.
My conscious self an open door,
for manifesting what is more.

I see that healing must begin
by finding Living Christ within.
For as I see with single eye,
each cell the light does amplify.

O Mother Mary, generate,
the song that does accelerate,
my cells into a higher state,
in perfect health they scintillate.

5. I know I am from heaven sent,
my bodies four the instrument,
through which the melody I play,
that manifests a brand new day.

In Mother's music I am free,
from memories of a lesser me.
My vision in a perfect state,
that all my cells regenerate.

O Mother Mary, generate,
the song that does accelerate,
my cells into a higher state,
in perfect health they scintillate.

6. I now accept my higher will,
and thus my mission I fulfill.
Transformer of the cosmic light,
I manifest my sacred right.

O Mother's Love, sweet melody,
from imperfections I AM free.
O Mother Mary, sound of sounds,
within my heart your love abounds.

O Mother Mary, generate,
the song that does accelerate,
my cells into a higher state,
in perfect health they scintillate.

7. My victory by Christ foretold,
my plan divine I see unfold.
Tween God and man no longer rift,
I manifest my highest gift.

Through Mother's beauty so sublime,
transcending bounds of space and time.
All cells beyond the mortal tomb,
as they are whole in Mother's womb.

O Mother Mary, generate,
the song that does accelerate,
my cells into a higher state,
in perfect health they scintillate.

8. As I surrender all that's "mine,"
no thing can block my plan divine.
And thus my bodies are set free,
from fallacy of lesser "me."

In resonance with life's own song,
in life's harmonics I belong.
The blueprint of my perfect state
does every cell reconsecrate.

O Mother Mary, generate,
the song that does accelerate,
my cells into a higher state,
in perfect health they scintillate.

9. In nexus of the figure-eight,
I am the fully open gate.
The Golden Age is given birth,
transfigured is our planet earth.

The tuning fork in every cell
is now attuned to Mother's bell.
From curse of death I AM now free,
I claim my immortality.

O Mother Mary, generate,
the song that does accelerate,
my cells into a higher state,
in perfect health they scintillate.

OM AH HUM,
MA-RAY GURU PADME SIDDHI HUM

(Chant 9X, 33X or more)

Sealing

In the name of the Divine Mother, I call to Mother Mary for the sealing of myself and all people in my circle of influence in the creative flow of the Divine Mother, the River of Life. I call for the multiplication of my calls by all representatives of the Divine Mother, so that we form the perfect figure-eight flow of "As Above, so below." Thus, I accept that this is fully manifest, because the mouth of the Lord, the Divine Mother that I AM, has spoken it. Amen.

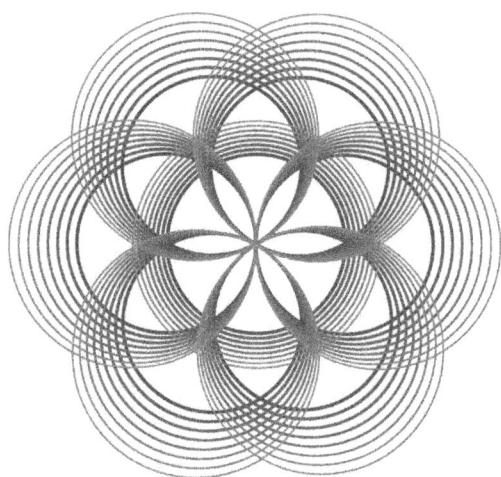

DECREE TO MOTHER MARY

In the name I AM THAT I AM, Jesus Christ, I call to all representatives of the Divine Mother, especially Mother Mary, for the healing of my four lower bodies, especially for the transfiguration of my physical body. I call for the healing of all imbalances and diseases, including...

[Make personal calls.]

1. O Blessed Mary's Song of Life,
consuming every form of strife.
As I attune to sound so fair,
each cell is healthy, I declare.

**O Mother Mary, generate,
the song that does accelerate,
my cells into a higher state,
in perfect health they scintillate.**

2. As life's own song I ever hear,
it does consume all sense of fear.
In tune with Mother's symphony,
from all diseases I AM free.

**O Mother Mary, generate,
the song that does accelerate,
my cells into a higher state,
in perfect health they scintillate.**

3. In Mother's love I do transcend,
and all my struggles hereby end.
For when with Mother's eye I see,
no imperfection touches me.

O Mother Mary, generate,
the song that does accelerate,
my cells into a higher state,
in perfect health they scintillate.

4. I see that healing must begin
by finding Living Christ within.
For as I see with single eye,
each cell the light does amplify.

O Mother Mary, generate,
the song that does accelerate,
my cells into a higher state,
in perfect health they scintillate.

5. In Mother's music I am free,
from memories of a lesser me.
My vision in a perfect state,
that all my cells regenerate.

O Mother Mary, generate,
the song that does accelerate,
my cells into a higher state,
in perfect health they scintillate.

6. O Mother's Love, sweet melody,
from imperfections I AM free.
O Mother Mary, sound of sounds,
within my heart your love abounds.

O Mother Mary, generate,
the song that does accelerate,
my cells into a higher state,
in perfect health they scintillate.

7. Through Mother's beauty so sublime,
transcending bounds of space and time.
All cells beyond the mortal tomb,
as they are whole in Mother's womb.

O Mother Mary, generate,
the song that does accelerate,
my cells into a higher state,
in perfect health they scintillate.

8. In resonance with life's own song,
in life's harmonics I belong.
The blueprint of my perfect state
does every cell reconsecrate.

O Mother Mary, generate,
the song that does accelerate,
my cells into a higher state,
in perfect health they scintillate.

9. The tuning fork in every cell
is now attuned to Mother's bell.
From curse of death I AM now free,
I claim my immortality.

O Mother Mary, generate,
the song that does accelerate,
my cells into a higher state,
in perfect health they scintillate.

Sealing

In the name of the Divine Mother, I call to Mother Mary for the sealing of myself and all people in my circle of influence in the creative flow of the Divine Mother, the River of Life. I call for the multiplication of my calls by all representatives of the Divine Mother, so that we form the perfect figure-eight flow of "As Above, so below." Thus, I accept that this is fully manifest, because the mouth of the Lord, the Divine Mother that I AM, has spoken it. Amen.

Song of Life 5

MANIFESTATION

In the name I AM THAT I AM, Jesus Christ, I call to all representatives of the Divine Mother, especially Portia and Mother Mary, for the healing of my four lower bodies, especially for the transfiguration of my world view. Help me fully surrender myself into the Cosmic Flow, so I can transcend the consciousness of lack and be led by the Holy Spirit to the places and circumstances where I can be of greatest service to the cause of raising all life. I call for the healing of all imbalances, including...

[Make personal calls.]

> When Father-Mother are as One,
> I see the rising of the Son.
> My Christic balance is the key,
> extremes they cannot capture me.

> When I am centered in the One,
> my inner balance I have won.
> My I AM Presence now can do,
> all that it wants through Conscious You.

When I have balanced Yang and Yin,
the victory of Christ I win.
As Mara's demons I transcend,
the eightfold path I do ascend.

When I complete the sacred quest,
fulfilling every subtle test.
With Jesus I the ghost release,
Gautama Buddha shows me peace.

When with Maitreya I am free,
Sanat Kumara greeting me.
Alpha-Omega are now one,
I am with them in Central Sun.

When nexus of their figure-eight,
opens up the cosmic gate.
With my Creator I can be,
I AM in true polarity.

When I return to planet earth,
a brand new Self is given birth.
I know now what for all is best,
the Will of God is manifest.

1. I am in Mother's flow

1. Of Mother's body I am part,
I am a child of Mother's Heart.
My I AM Presence in control,
I now accept my rightful role.

O Portia, in your own retreat,
with Mother's Love you do me greet.
As all my tests I now complete,
old patterns I no more repeat.

O Portia, opportunity,
I am beyond duality.
I focus now internally,
with you I grow eternally.

2. I will no more sit idly by,
no forces can me pacify.
I claim my place in Mother's flow,
all problems I will now outgrow.

O Portia, Justice is your name,
upholding Cosmic Honor Flame,
No longer will I play the game,
of seeking to remain the same.

O Portia, opportunity,
I am beyond duality.
I focus now internally,
with you I grow eternally.

3. As cosmic movement I now see,
I know a new reality.
When dual vision I reject,
no problems that I need correct.

O Portia, in the cosmic flow,
one with you, I ever grow.
I am the chalice here below,
of cosmic justice you bestow.

O Portia, opportunity,
I am beyond duality.
I focus now internally,
with you I grow eternally.

4. The force-based mindset I transcend,
the ego I need not defend.
I'm free from the eternal foe,
as I now redirect the flow.

O Portia, cosmic balance bring,
eternal hope, my heart does sing.
Protected by your Mother's wing,
I feel at one with everything.

O Portia, opportunity,
I am beyond duality.
I focus now internally,
with you I grow eternally.

5. As I attune to cosmic sound,
my Spirit is not matter bound.
I now decide to change my course,
by moving back towards my source.

O Portia, bring the Mother Light,
to set all free from darkest night.
Your Love Flame shines forever bright,
with Saint Germain now hold me tight.

**O Portia, opportunity,
I am beyond duality.
I focus now internally,
with you I grow eternally.**

6. No choice I ever made before,
has power over me no more.
When I let go of spirits old,
my future not by past foretold.

O Portia, in your mastery,
I feel transforming chemistry.
In your light of reality,
I find the golden alchemy.

**O Portia, opportunity,
I am beyond duality.
I focus now internally,
with you I grow eternally.**

7. For Cosmic Justice does decree,
that from my past I can be free.
As single vision I now find,
Goddess of Justice no more blind.

O Portia, in the cosmic stream,
I am awake from human dream.
Removing now the ego's beam,
I earn my place on cosmic team.

O Portia, opportunity,
I am beyond duality.
I focus now internally,
with you I grow eternally.

8. Instead I see with balanced eyes,
exposing dualistic lies.
To spirits old I hereby shout,
commanding them to come on out.

O Portia, you come from afar,
you are a cosmic avatar.
So infinite your repertoire,
you are for earth a guiding star.

O Portia, opportunity,
I am beyond duality.
I focus now internally,
with you I grow eternally.

9. Remaking each unbalanced choice,
my scales in balance, I rejoice.
With Portia I the matrix shatter,
my Spirit not entombed in matter.

O Portia, I am confident,
I am a cosmic instrument.
I came to earth from heaven sent,
to help bring forward her ascent.

O Portia, opportunity,
I am beyond duality.
I focus now internally,
with you I grow eternally.

2. Flowing with the cosmic dance

1. God has no need to punish me,
God's Justice wants me to be free.
Yet freedom means to balance find,
so I attain the single mind.

O Portia, in your own retreat,
with Mother's Love you do me greet.
As all my tests I now complete,
old patterns I no more repeat.

O Portia, opportunity,
I am beyond duality.
I focus now internally,
with you I grow eternally.

2. With Portia as my loving guide,
old spirits can no longer hide.
As I now balance my own scale,
the Holy Spirit fills my sail.

O Portia, Justice is your name,
upholding Cosmic Honor Flame,
No longer will I play the game,
of seeking to remain the same.

O Portia, opportunity,
I am beyond duality.
I focus now internally,
with you I grow eternally.

3. Wher'er the winds of Spirit blow,
I just surrender to the flow.
The Spirit is now leading me,
to where I can of service be.

O Portia, in the cosmic flow,
one with you, I ever grow.
I am the chalice here below,
of cosmic justice you bestow.

O Portia, opportunity,
I am beyond duality.
I focus now internally,
with you I grow eternally.

4. No longer bound by circumstance,
I flow along with cosmic dance.
Where Spirit points, I gladly go,
I seek to help all people grow.

O Portia, cosmic balance bring,
eternal hope, my heart does sing.
Protected by your Mother's wing,
I feel at one with everything.

O Portia, opportunity,
I am beyond duality.
I focus now internally,
with you I grow eternally.

5. My Conscious You an open door,
for all my Presence has in store.
In bringing forth the Spirit's gift,
I only seek all life to lift.

O Portia, bring the Mother Light,
to set all free from darkest night.
Your Love Flame shines forever bright,
with Saint Germain now hold me tight.

O Portia, opportunity,
I am beyond duality.
I focus now internally,
with you I grow eternally.

6. In selfless service, "I" am lost,
counting not the human cost.
As higher purpose I now find,
all hindrances I leave behind.

O Portia, in your mastery,
I feel transforming chemistry.
In your light of reality,
I find the golden alchemy.

**O Portia, opportunity,
I am beyond duality.
I focus now internally,
with you I grow eternally.**

7. I seize the opportunity,
to enter higher unity.
I'm part of the Ascended Host,
my service is what matters most.

O Portia, in the cosmic stream,
I am awake from human dream.
Removing now the ego's beam,
I earn my place on cosmic team.

**O Portia, opportunity,
I am beyond duality.
I focus now internally,
with you I grow eternally.**

8. Ascended masters on my team,
the earth for God we will redeem.
The force of master's rising wave,
frees people from platonic cave.

O Portia, you come from afar,
you are a cosmic avatar.
So infinite your repertoire,
you are for earth a guiding star.

O Portia, opportunity,
I am beyond duality.
I focus now internally,
with you I grow eternally.

9. The masters through me light bestow,
and as above is all below.
As Cosmic Light we do disperse,
we raise the matter universe.

O Portia, I am confident,
I am a cosmic instrument.
I came to earth from heaven sent,
to help bring forward her ascent.

O Portia, opportunity,
I am beyond duality.
I focus now internally,
with you I grow eternally.

3. I invoke Cosmic Justice

1. If fallen beings me attack,
their energies I mirror back.
For I join forces with the meek,
who always turn the other cheek.

O Portia, in your own retreat,
with Mother's Love you do me greet.
As all my tests I now complete,
old patterns I no more repeat.

O Portia, opportunity,
I am beyond duality.
I focus now internally,
with you I grow eternally.

2. Resist not evil is the call,
redeeming us from cosmic fall.
Extending opportunity,
to beings outside unity.

O Portia, Justice is your name,
upholding Cosmic Honor Flame,
No longer will I play the game,
of seeking to remain the same.

O Portia, opportunity,
I am beyond duality.
I focus now internally,
with you I grow eternally.

3. To those with serpent's vicious sting,
let Christ in me the judgment bring.
Let earth be free from downward pull,
of those who are of venom full.

O Portia, in the cosmic flow,
one with you, I ever grow.
I am the chalice here below,
of cosmic justice you bestow.

O Portia, opportunity,
I am beyond duality.
I focus now internally,
with you I grow eternally.

4. O Portia, Cosmic Justice bring,
your angels Song of Justice sing.
As Portia judges fallen lot,
the earth is free from devil's plot.

O Portia, cosmic balance bring,
eternal hope, my heart does sing.
Protected by your Mother's wing,
I feel at one with everything.

O Portia, opportunity,
I am beyond duality.
I focus now internally,
with you I grow eternally.

5. As Mara's demons are all bound,
both peace and unity abound.
My heart now barely can contain,
the joy of greeting Saint Germain.

O Portia, bring the Mother Light,
to set all free from darkest night.
Your Love Flame shines forever bright,
with Saint Germain now hold me tight.

O Portia, opportunity,
I am beyond duality.
I focus now internally,
with you I grow eternally.

6. I am the nexus of the flow,
from God above to all below.
In flow of cosmic figure-eight,
I master's light reverberate.

O Portia, in your mastery,
I feel transforming chemistry.
In your light of reality,
I find the golden alchemy.

O Portia, opportunity,
I am beyond duality.
I focus now internally,
with you I grow eternally.

7. My plan divine I see unfold,
what wondrous beauty I behold.
I find my place in cosmic plan,
I bridge the gap tween God and man.

O Portia, in the cosmic stream,
I am awake from human dream.
Removing now the ego's beam,
I earn my place on cosmic team.

O Portia, opportunity,
I am beyond duality.
I focus now internally,
with you I grow eternally.

8. In unity with Presence mine,
I AM now letting my light shine.
My light is set upon an hill,
I'm using it with Christic skill.

O Portia, you come from afar,
you are a cosmic avatar.
So infinite your repertoire,
you are for earth a guiding star.

O Portia, opportunity,
I am beyond duality.
I focus now internally,
with you I grow eternally.

9. As I now see with single sight,
I do direct the sacred light.
The light transforms our planet earth,
the Golden Age is given birth.

O Portia, I am confident,
I am a cosmic instrument.
I came to earth from heaven sent,
to help bring forward her ascent.

O Portia, opportunity,
I am beyond duality.
I focus now internally,
with you I grow eternally.

4. I manifest my divine plan

1. Unfolding for my inner sight,
my plan divine now comes to light.
I effortlessly join the flow,
towards my goal I ever grow.

O Portia, in your own retreat,
with Mother's Love you do me greet.
As all my tests I now complete,
old patterns I no more repeat.

O Portia, opportunity,
I am beyond duality.
I focus now internally,
with you I grow eternally.

2. The universe does manifest,
all that I need to do my best.
I now accept my perfect health,
I now accept abundant wealth.

O Portia, Justice is your name,
upholding Cosmic Honor Flame,
No longer will I play the game,
of seeking to remain the same.

**O Portia, opportunity,
I am beyond duality.
I focus now internally,
with you I grow eternally.**

3. Transcending consciousness of lack,
the joy of life is fully back.
I now accept my inner peace,
I now accept that war will cease.

O Portia, in the cosmic flow,
one with you, I ever grow.
I am the chalice here below,
of cosmic justice you bestow.

**O Portia, opportunity,
I am beyond duality.
I focus now internally,
with you I grow eternally.**

4. As master's lessons I have learned,
I know the cosmic tide has turned.
I now accept the Christic mind,
I now accept a life refined.

O Portia, cosmic balance bring,
eternal hope, my heart does sing.
Protected by your Mother's wing,
I feel at one with everything.

**O Portia, opportunity,
I am beyond duality.
I focus now internally,
with you I grow eternally.**

5. As I am ever moving up,
I know my progress will not stop.
I now accept my perfect place,
I now accept more Cosmic Grace.

O Portia, bring the Mother Light,
to set all free from darkest night.
Your Love Flame shines forever bright,
with Saint Germain now hold me tight.

**O Portia, opportunity,
I am beyond duality.
I focus now internally,
with you I grow eternally.**

6. I am a cosmic optimist,
for ego, I'm an exorcist.
I now accept that God provides,
I now accept the rising tides.

O Portia, in your mastery,
I feel transforming chemistry.
In your light of reality,
I find the golden alchemy.

O Portia, opportunity,
I am beyond duality.
I focus now internally,
with you I grow eternally.

7. As I remain the open door,
I always will receive what's more.
I now accept my innocence,
I now accept God's opulence.

O Portia, in the cosmic stream,
I am awake from human dream.
Removing now the ego's beam,
I earn my place on cosmic team.

O Portia, opportunity,
I am beyond duality.
I focus now internally,
with you I grow eternally.

8. I mirror all that is above,
and thus I radiate pure love.
I now accept that I am free,
I now accept the Christic me.

O Portia, you come from afar,
you are a cosmic avatar.
So infinite your repertoire,
you are for earth a guiding star.

O Portia, opportunity,
I am beyond duality.
I focus now internally,
with you I grow eternally.

9. With Portia I'm in unity,
I seize the opportunity.
I now accept divine excess,
I now accept my full success.

O Portia, I am confident,
I am a cosmic instrument.
I came to earth from heaven sent,
to help bring forward her ascent.

O Portia, opportunity,
I am beyond duality.
I focus now internally,
with you I grow eternally.

OM AH HUM,
PORTIA GURU PADME SIDDHI HUM

(Chant 9X, 33X or more)

Sealing

In the name of the Divine Mother, I call to Portia and Mother Mary for the sealing of myself and all people in my circle of influence in the creative flow of the Divine Mother, the River of Life. I call for the multiplication of my calls by all representatives of the Divine Mother, so that we form the perfect figure-eight flow of "As Above, so below." Thus, I accept that this is fully manifest, because the mouth of the Lord, the Divine Mother that I AM, has spoken it. Amen.

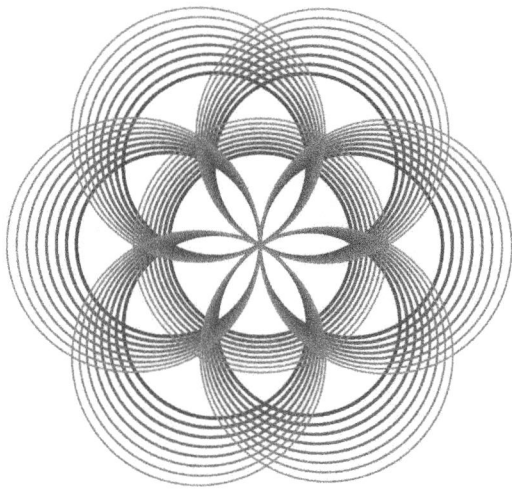

DECREE TO PORTIA

In the name I AM THAT I AM, Jesus Christ, I call to all representatives of the Divine Mother, especially Portia and Mother Mary, for the healing of my four lower bodies, especially for the transfiguration of my world view. Help me fully surrender myself into the Cosmic Flow, so I can transcend the consciousness of lack and be led by the Holy Spirit to the places and circumstances where I can be of greatest service to the cause of raising all life. I call for the healing of all imbalances, including...

[Make personal calls.]

1. O Portia, in your own retreat,
with Mother's Love you do me greet.
As all my tests I now complete,
old patterns I no more repeat.

O Portia, opportunity,
I am beyond duality.
I focus now internally,
with you I grow eternally.

2. O Portia, Justice is your name,
upholding Cosmic Honor Flame,
No longer will I play the game,
of seeking to remain the same.

O Portia, opportunity,
I am beyond duality.
I focus now internally,
with you I grow eternally.

3. O Portia, in the cosmic flow,
one with you, I ever grow.
I am the chalice here below,
of cosmic justice you bestow.

O Portia, opportunity,
I am beyond duality.
I focus now internally,
with you I grow eternally.

4. O Portia, cosmic balance bring,
eternal hope, my heart does sing.
Protected by your Mother's wing,
I feel at one with everything.

O Portia, opportunity,
I am beyond duality.
I focus now internally,
with you I grow eternally.

5. O Portia, bring the Mother Light,
to set all free from darkest night.
Your Love Flame shines forever bright,
with Saint Germain now hold me tight.

O Portia, opportunity,
I am beyond duality.
I focus now internally,
with you I grow eternally.

6. O Portia, in your mastery,
I feel transforming chemistry.
In your light of reality,
I find the golden alchemy.

O Portia, opportunity,
I am beyond duality.
I focus now internally,
with you I grow eternally.

7. O Portia, in the cosmic stream,
I am awake from human dream.
Removing now the ego's beam,
I earn my place on cosmic team.

O Portia, opportunity,
I am beyond duality.
I focus now internally,
with you I grow eternally.

8. O Portia, you come from afar,
you are a cosmic avatar.
So infinite your repertoire,
you are for earth a guiding star.

**O Portia, opportunity,
I am beyond duality.
I focus now internally,
with you I grow eternally.**

9. O Portia, I am confident,
I am a cosmic instrument.
I came to earth from heaven sent,
to help bring forward her ascent.

**O Portia, opportunity,
I am beyond duality.
I focus now internally,
with you I grow eternally.**

Sealing

In the name of the Divine Mother, I call to Portia and Mother Mary for the sealing of myself and all people in my circle of influence in the creative flow of the Divine Mother, the River of Life. I call for the multiplication of my calls by all representatives of the Divine Mother, so that we form the perfect figure-eight flow of "As Above, so below." Thus, I accept that this is fully manifest, because the mouth of the Lord, the Divine Mother that I AM, has spoken it. Amen.

Song of Life 6

ABUNDANCE

In the name I AM THAT I AM, Jesus Christ, I call to all representatives of the Divine Mother, especially Goddess of Liberty and Mother Mary, for the healing of my four lower bodies, especially for the transfiguration of my freedom to create, including the manifestation of the abundant life. I call for the healing of all sense of poverty and lack, including…

[Make personal calls.]

When Father-Mother are as One,
I see the rising of the Son.
My Christic balance is the key,
extremes they cannot capture me.

When I am centered in the One,
my inner balance I have won.
My I AM Presence now can do,
all that it wants through Conscious You.

When I have balanced Yang and Yin,
the victory of Christ I win.
As Mara's demons I transcend,
the eightfold path I do ascend.

When I complete the sacred quest,
fulfilling every subtle test.
With Jesus I the ghost release,
Gautama Buddha shows me peace.

When with Maitreya I am free,
Sanat Kumara greeting me.
Alpha-Omega are now one,
I am with them in Central Sun.

When nexus of their figure-eight,
opens up the cosmic gate.
With my Creator I can be,
I AM in true polarity.

When I return to planet earth,
a brand new Self is given birth.
I know now what for all is best,
the Will of God is manifest.

1. I surrender hatred of Mother

1. O Cosmic Mother Liberty,
there is no greater love I see.
Transcending lack and poverty,
of you I am a devotee.

O Liberty now set me free
from devil's curse of poverty.
I blame not Mother for my lack,
O Blessed Mother, take me back.

**O Cosmic Mother Liberty,
conduct Abundance Symphony.
My highest service I now see,
abundance is now real for me.**

2. Of oneness I was in pursuit,
but then I ate forbidden fruit.
Believing in the serpent's plot,
reality I then forgot.

O Liberty, from distant shore,
I come with longing to be More.
I see abundance is a flow,
abundance consciousness I grow.

**O Cosmic Mother Liberty,
conduct Abundance Symphony.
My highest service I now see,
abundance is now real for me.**

3. And suddenly the world did change,
indeed, it was so very strange.
The Mother did now seem to be,
only out to punish me.

O Liberty, expose the lie,
that limitations can me tie.
The Ma-ter light is not my foe,
true opulence it does bestow.

O Cosmic Mother Liberty,
conduct Abundance Symphony.
My highest service I now see,
abundance is now real for me.

4. The cosmic mirror would reflect,
whatever that I did project.
As everything did now go wrong,
my sense of guilt was very strong.

O Liberty, expose the plot,
projected by the fallen lot.
O Cosmic Mother, I now see,
that Mother's not my enemy.

O Cosmic Mother Liberty,
conduct Abundance Symphony.
My highest service I now see,
abundance is now real for me.

5. In an attempt to compensate,
the ego I did now create.
To Conscious You it felt like hell,
I fled into my little shell.

O Liberty, with opened eyes,
I now reject the devil's lies.
I now embrace the Mother realm,
for I see Father at the helm.

**O Cosmic Mother Liberty,
conduct Abundance Symphony.
My highest service I now see,
abundance is now real for me.**

6. With ego running now the show,
I was apart from life's own flow.
The Mother kept on sending back,
what seemed to me like an attack.

O Liberty, a chalice pure,
my lower bodies are for sure.
Release through me your symphony,
your gift of Cosmic Liberty.

**O Cosmic Mother Liberty,
conduct Abundance Symphony.
My highest service I now see,
abundance is now real for me.**

7. I felt condemned the world to roam,
often wanting to go home.
It seemed like it was all too late,
for Mother I felt only hate.

O Liberty, the open door,
I am for Symphony of More.
In chakras mine light you release,
the flow of love shall never cease.

O Cosmic Mother Liberty,
conduct Abundance Symphony.
My highest service I now see,
abundance is now real for me.

8. Yet suddenly, a flash of light,
the Starry Mother shining bright.
It was my Mother Liberty,
sending Christic Light to me.

O Liberty, release the flow,
of opulence that you bestow.
For I am willing to receive,
the Golden Fleece that you now weave.

O Cosmic Mother Liberty,
conduct Abundance Symphony.
My highest service I now see,
abundance is now real for me.

9. The scales now falling from my eye,
the Mother's love I can't deny.
She shows me that I can return,
when ego-bridges I will burn.

O Liberty, release the cure,
to free the tired and the poor.
The huddled masses are set free,
by loving Song of Liberty.

O Cosmic Mother Liberty,
conduct Abundance Symphony.
My highest service I now see,
abundance is now real for me.

2. I accept Mother's abundance

1. O Cosmic Mother Liberty,
from serpent's lie I am set free.
I see that Mother is my friend,
on her support I can depend.

O Liberty now set me free
from devil's curse of poverty.
I blame not Mother for my lack,
O Blessed Mother, take me back.

O Cosmic Mother Liberty,
conduct Abundance Symphony.
My highest service I now see,
abundance is now real for me.

2. When I transcend the sense of strife,
she will give me abundant life.
For Mother loves to manifest,
what is for me the very best.

O Liberty, from distant shore,
I come with longing to be More.
I see abundance is a flow,
abundance consciousness I grow.

**O Cosmic Mother Liberty,
conduct Abundance Symphony.
My highest service I now see,
abundance is now real for me.**

3. Yet for abundance to receive,
I must my innocence retrieve.
For childlike mind is master key,
to flowing with God's alchemy.

O Liberty, expose the lie,
that limitations can me tie.
The Ma-ter light is not my foe,
true opulence it does bestow.

**O Cosmic Mother Liberty,
conduct Abundance Symphony.
My highest service I now see,
abundance is now real for me.**

4. For if I set out to deceive,
success I never will achieve.
And if I heaven take by force,
I separate myself from Source.

O Liberty, expose the plot,
projected by the fallen lot.
O Cosmic Mother, I now see,
that Mother's not my enemy.

O Cosmic Mother Liberty,
conduct Abundance Symphony.
My highest service I now see,
abundance is now real for me.

5. But when with childlike mind I play,
I co-create a brand new day.
The Ma-ter light I do set free,
to give abundance unto me.

O Liberty, with opened eyes,
I now reject the devil's lies.
I now embrace the Mother realm,
for I see Father at the helm.

O Cosmic Mother Liberty,
conduct Abundance Symphony.
My highest service I now see,
abundance is now real for me.

6. When Christ in me rebukes the storm,
abundance truly is the norm.
When Elohim designed the earth,
to perfect matrix they gave birth.

O Liberty, a chalice pure,
my lower bodies are for sure.
Release through me your symphony,
your gift of Cosmic Liberty.

**O Cosmic Mother Liberty,
conduct Abundance Symphony.
My highest service I now see,
abundance is now real for me.**

7. When Christlike mind is my pursuit,
my garden bears abundant fruit.
I do receive God's opulence,
with none of human decadence.

O Liberty, the open door,
I am for Symphony of More.
In chakras mine light you release,
the flow of love shall never cease.

**O Cosmic Mother Liberty,
conduct Abundance Symphony.
My highest service I now see,
abundance is now real for me.**

8. When force-based mindset I give up,
my heart becomes a Holy Cup.
And as I raise the chalice pure,
the Life of Christ is mine for sure.

O Liberty, release the flow,
of opulence that you bestow.
For I am willing to receive,
the Golden Fleece that you now weave.

**O Cosmic Mother Liberty,
conduct Abundance Symphony.
My highest service I now see,
abundance is now real for me.**

9. For as I now take up my cross,
the death of spirits is no loss.
With Christ I am reborn of fire,
my vision raising ever higher.

O Liberty, release the cure,
to free the tired and the poor.
The huddled masses are set free,
by loving Song of Liberty.

**O Cosmic Mother Liberty,
conduct Abundance Symphony.
My highest service I now see,
abundance is now real for me.**

3. I receive Mother's ideas

1. O blessed Mother Liberty,
in cosmic service I am free.
Abundance Mother wants to give,
to all who on this planet live.

O Liberty now set me free
from devil's curse of poverty.
I blame not Mother for my lack,
O Blessed Mother, take me back.

O Cosmic Mother Liberty,
conduct Abundance Symphony.
My highest service I now see,
abundance is now real for me.

2. And when I do not seek to own,
I do attune to Cosmic Tone.
As I become the open door,
the Flow of Life we do restore.

O Liberty, from distant shore,
I come with longing to be More.
I see abundance is a flow,
abundance consciousness I grow.

O Cosmic Mother Liberty,
conduct Abundance Symphony.
My highest service I now see,
abundance is now real for me.

3. As I with single eye perceive,
ideas new I do receive.
All sense of lack I do transcend,
as Mother's love all wounds will mend.

O Liberty, expose the lie,
that limitations can me tie.
The Ma-ter light is not my foe,
true opulence it does bestow.

**O Cosmic Mother Liberty,
conduct Abundance Symphony.
My highest service I now see,
abundance is now real for me.**

4. I will receive as I do give,
in this awareness I now live.
And thus I seek all life to raise,
for self-awareness I give praise.

O Liberty, expose the plot,
projected by the fallen lot.
O Cosmic Mother, I now see,
that Mother's not my enemy.

**O Cosmic Mother Liberty,
conduct Abundance Symphony.
My highest service I now see,
abundance is now real for me.**

5. My gratitude I give to thee,
for cosmic opportunity.
As I surrender what is old,
a golden future I behold.

O Liberty, with opened eyes,
I now reject the devil's lies.
I now embrace the Mother realm,
for I see Father at the helm.

O Cosmic Mother Liberty,
conduct Abundance Symphony.
My highest service I now see,
abundance is now real for me.

6. As I become a Christic knight,
I fully love the Mother Light.
I am now pure as sacred lamb,
a part of Mother, this I am.

O Liberty, a chalice pure,
my lower bodies are for sure.
Release through me your symphony,
your gift of Cosmic Liberty.

O Cosmic Mother Liberty,
conduct Abundance Symphony.
My highest service I now see,
abundance is now real for me.

7. The Sacred Flow we do restore,
we bring to earth all that is More.
We follow ancient Mother's call,
as nurturance we give to all.

O Liberty, the open door,
I am for Symphony of More.
In chakras mine light you release,
the flow of love shall never cease.

**O Cosmic Mother Liberty,
conduct Abundance Symphony.
My highest service I now see,
abundance is now real for me.**

8. As I am in my rightful place,
now flows through me my Mother's Grace.
As all are filled with Mother's gift,
from fear to love they start to shift.

O Liberty, release the flow,
of opulence that you bestow.
For I am willing to receive,
the Golden Fleece that you now weave.

**O Cosmic Mother Liberty,
conduct Abundance Symphony.
My highest service I now see,
abundance is now real for me.**

9. Perhaps the greatest gift of all,
is that we can transcend the fall.
As we accept that we are one,
the Age of Mother has begun.

O Liberty, release the cure,
to free the tired and the poor.
The huddled masses are set free,
by loving Song of Liberty.

**O Cosmic Mother Liberty,
conduct Abundance Symphony.
My highest service I now see,
abundance is now real for me.**

4. I accept Mother's wealth

1. O blessed Mother Liberty,
release the wealth to set all free.
Let nature spirits now be healed,
let nature's riches be revealed.

O Liberty now set me free
from devil's curse of poverty.
I blame not Mother for my lack,
O Blessed Mother, take me back.

**O Cosmic Mother Liberty,
conduct Abundance Symphony.
My highest service I now see,
abundance is now real for me.**

2. A Horn of Plenty, Mother Earth,
to cosmic bounty she gives birth.
Abundant crops will spring from soil,
relieving people of their toil.

O Liberty, from distant shore,
I come with longing to be More.
I see abundance is a flow,
abundance consciousness I grow.

**O Cosmic Mother Liberty,
conduct Abundance Symphony.
My highest service I now see,
abundance is now real for me.**

3. No child shall ever hunger here,
no mother ever live in fear.
We rise above self-interest,
abundant life now manifest.

O Liberty, expose the lie,
that limitations can me tie.
The Ma-ter light is not my foe,
true opulence it does bestow.

**O Cosmic Mother Liberty,
conduct Abundance Symphony.
My highest service I now see,
abundance is now real for me.**

4. All those who seek an unfair share,
of Christic judgment should beware.
Let them all know that time is up,
all selfishness they must now stop.

O Liberty, expose the plot,
projected by the fallen lot.
O Cosmic Mother, I now see,
that Mother's not my enemy.

**O Cosmic Mother Liberty,
conduct Abundance Symphony.
My highest service I now see,
abundance is now real for me.**

5. For earth is given to the meek,
all those who oneness truly seek.
With Christ in unity we stand,
equality we now demand.

O Liberty, with opened eyes,
I now reject the devil's lies.
I now embrace the Mother realm,
for I see Father at the helm.

**O Cosmic Mother Liberty,
conduct Abundance Symphony.
My highest service I now see,
abundance is now real for me.**

6. The Law of God is most profound,
the Ma-ter light by law is bound.
Whatever we in love do ask,
the Mother is up to the task.

O Liberty, a chalice pure,
my lower bodies are for sure.
Release through me your symphony,
your gift of Cosmic Liberty.

**O Cosmic Mother Liberty,
conduct Abundance Symphony.
My highest service I now see,
abundance is now real for me.**

7. The Mother Light just loves to bring,
abundant gifts to make hearts sing.
And thus with Christ we hereby call,
God's kingdom manifest for all.

O Liberty, the open door,
I am for Symphony of More.
In chakras mine light you release,
the flow of love shall never cease.

**O Cosmic Mother Liberty,
conduct Abundance Symphony.
My highest service I now see,
abundance is now real for me.**

8. As Cosmic Law we do employ,
all hearts will sing an ode to joy.
This planet finally will be,
the paradise God wants to see.

O Liberty, release the flow,
of opulence that you bestow.
For I am willing to receive,
the Golden Fleece that you now weave.

**O Cosmic Mother Liberty,
conduct Abundance Symphony.
My highest service I now see,
abundance is now real for me.**

9. O Blessed Mother Liberty,
we hum your cosmic melody.
We know that we are one with thee,
and thus we truly are carefree.

O Liberty, release the cure,
to free the tired and the poor.
The huddled masses are set free,
by loving Song of Liberty.

**O Cosmic Mother Liberty,
conduct Abundance Symphony.
My highest service I now see,
abundance is now real for me.**

**OM AH HUM,
LIBERTY GURU PADME SIDDHI HUM**

(Chant 9X, 33X or more)

Sealing

In the name of the Divine Mother, I call to Goddess of Liberty and Mother Mary for the sealing of myself and all people in my circle of influence in the creative flow of the Divine Mother, the River of Life. I call for the multiplication of my calls by all representatives of the Divine Mother, so that we form the perfect figure-eight flow of "As Above, so below." Thus, I accept that this is fully manifest, because the mouth of the Lord, the Divine Mother that I AM, has spoken it. Amen.

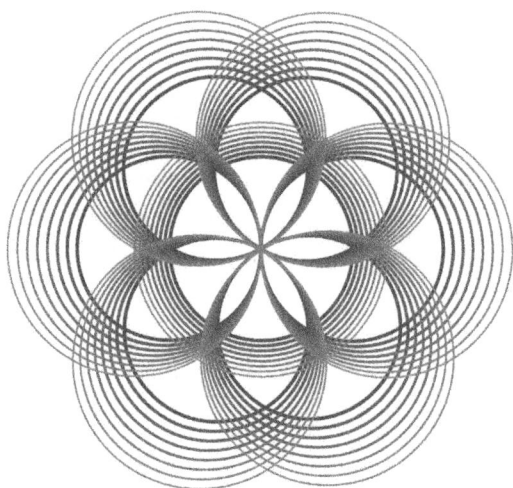

DECREE TO LIBERTY

In the name I AM THAT I AM, Jesus Christ, I call to all representatives of the Divine Mother, especially Goddess of Liberty and Mother Mary, for the healing of my four lower bodies, especially for the transfiguration of my freedom to create, including the manifestation of the abundant life. I call for the healing of all sense of poverty and lack, including...

[Make personal calls.]

1. O Liberty now set me free
from devil's curse of poverty.
I blame not Mother for my lack,
O Blessed Mother, take me back.

**O Cosmic Mother Liberty,
conduct Abundance Symphony.
My highest service I now see,
abundance is now real for me.**

2. O Liberty, from distant shore,
I come with longing to be More.
I see abundance is a flow,
abundance consciousness I grow.

**O Cosmic Mother Liberty,
conduct Abundance Symphony.
My highest service I now see,
abundance is now real for me.**

3. O Liberty, expose the lie,
that limitations can me tie.
The Ma-ter light is not my foe,
true opulence it does bestow.

**O Cosmic Mother Liberty,
conduct Abundance Symphony.
My highest service I now see,
abundance is now real for me.**

4. O Liberty, expose the plot,
projected by the fallen lot.
O Cosmic Mother, I now see,
that Mother's not my enemy.

**O Cosmic Mother Liberty,
conduct Abundance Symphony.
My highest service I now see,
abundance is now real for me.**

5. O Liberty, with opened eyes,
I now reject the devil's lies.
I now embrace the Mother realm,
for I see Father at the helm.

O Cosmic Mother Liberty,
conduct Abundance Symphony.
My highest service I now see,
abundance is now real for me.

6. O Liberty, a chalice pure,
my lower bodies are for sure.
Release through me your symphony,
your gift of Cosmic Liberty.

O Cosmic Mother Liberty,
conduct Abundance Symphony.
My highest service I now see,
abundance is now real for me.

7. O Liberty, the open door,
I am for Symphony of More.
In chakras mine light you release,
the flow of love shall never cease.

O Cosmic Mother Liberty,
conduct Abundance Symphony.
My highest service I now see,
abundance is now real for me.

8. O Liberty, release the flow,
of opulence that you bestow.
For I am willing to receive,
the Golden Fleece that you now weave.

**O Cosmic Mother Liberty,
conduct Abundance Symphony.
My highest service I now see,
abundance is now real for me.**

9. O Liberty, release the cure,
to free the tired and the poor.
The huddled masses are set free,
by loving Song of Liberty.

**O Cosmic Mother Liberty,
conduct Abundance Symphony.
My highest service I now see,
abundance is now real for me.**

Sealing

In the name of the Divine Mother, I call to Goddess of Liberty and Mother Mary for the sealing of myself and all people in my circle of influence in the creative flow of the Divine Mother, the River of Life. I call for the multiplication of my calls by all representatives of the Divine Mother, so that we form the perfect figure-eight flow of "As Above, so below." Thus, I accept that this is fully manifest, because the mouth of the Lord, the Divine Mother that I AM, has spoken it. Amen.

Song of Life 7

LOVING FLOW

In the name I AM THAT I AM, Jesus Christ, I call to all representatives of the Divine Mother, especially Lady Master Venus and Mother Mary, for the healing of my four lower bodies, especially for the transfiguration of my ability to accept unconditional love and let it flow through me. I call for the healing of all forms of conditional love, including...

[Make personal calls.]

> When Father-Mother are as One,
> I see the rising of the Son.
> My Christic balance is the key,
> extremes they cannot capture me.

> When I am centered in the One,
> my inner balance I have won.
> My I AM Presence now can do,
> all that it wants through Conscious You.

> When I have balanced Yang and Yin,
> the victory of Christ I win.
> As Mara's demons I transcend,
> the eightfold path I do ascend.

When I complete the sacred quest,
fulfilling every subtle test.
With Jesus I the ghost release,
Gautama Buddha shows me peace.

When with Maitreya I am free,
Sanat Kumara greeting me.
Alpha-Omega are now one,
I am with them in Central Sun.

When nexus of their figure-eight,
opens up the cosmic gate.
With my Creator I can be,
I AM in true polarity.

When I return to planet earth,
a brand new Self is given birth.
I know now what for all is best,
the Will of God is manifest.

1. Why I came to earth

1. O Love, you motivate our God,
O Love, you are Creator's Rod.
O Love, you are the sacred sound,
O Love, you are all over found.

O Venus, show me how to serve,
your cosmic beauty I observe.
What love from Venus you now bring,
our planets do in tandem sing.

O Venus, service so divine,
you are for earth a cosmic sign.
Your selfless service is now mine,
a life in service I define.

2. In Love Sanat Kumara came,
to earth when she was black with shame.
When cosmic councils could not cope,
he said: I still hold on to hope.

O Venus, your love is the key,
the hardened hearts on earth are free.
Embracing future bright and bold,
our planet's story is retold.

O Venus, service so divine,
you are for earth a cosmic sign.
Your selfless service is now mine,
a life in service I define.

3. He came with Love to set earth free,
to be the star she's meant to be.
And many came with him to earth,
forgetting their venutian birth.

O Venus, loving Mother mine,
my heart your love does now refine.
I am the open door for love,
descending like a Holy Dove.

O Venus, service so divine,
you are for earth a cosmic sign.
Your selfless service is now mine,
a life in service I define.

4. They came to selfless service give,
they vowed to on this planet live.
They came from Morning Star above,
to darkened star devoid of Love.

O Venus, play the secret note,
that is for hatred antidote.
All poisoned hearts you gently heal,
as love's true story you reveal.

O Venus, service so divine,
you are for earth a cosmic sign.
Your selfless service is now mine,
a life in service I define.

5. When they first came, it was a shock,
to see how people Love did mock.
And many over time forgot,
succumbing to the serpent's plot.

O Venus, love fills every need,
for truly, love is God's first seed.
O let it blossom, let it grow,
sweep earth into your loving flow.

O Venus, service so divine,
you are for earth a cosmic sign.
Your selfless service is now mine,
a life in service I define.

6. Yet Venus helps me to wake up,
by pouring Love into my cup.
I am not here to be a slave,
of those trapped in platonic cave.

O Venus, music of the spheres,
heard by those who God reveres.
Our voices now as one we raise,
singing in adoring praise.

O Venus, service so divine,
you are for earth a cosmic sign.
Your selfless service is now mine,
a life in service I define.

7. I surely did not come from dust,
fulfill my destiny I must.
To dust I never will return,
for fiery Love all dross will burn.

O Venus, we are joining ranks,
Sanat Kumara we give thanks.
Our planet has received new life,
to lift her out of war and strife.

**O Venus, service so divine,
you are for earth a cosmic sign.
Your selfless service is now mine,
a life in service I define.**

8. I look up into firmament,
I see the Love Star that God sent.
And I accept the call to be,
Love's Messenger to set earth free.

O Venus, your sweet melody,
consumes veil of duality.
Absorbed in tones of Cosmic Love,
all conflict we now rise above.

**O Venus, service so divine,
you are for earth a cosmic sign.
Your selfless service is now mine,
a life in service I define.**

9. O Venus, now come graciously,
I want you to initiate me.
I want to be the open door,
Sanat Kumara was before.

O Venus, shining Morning Star,
a cosmic herald, that you are.
The earth set free by sacred sound,
our planet is now heaven-bound.

O Venus, service so divine,
you are for earth a cosmic sign.
Your selfless service is now mine,
a life in service I define.

2. I want to know love

1. I now step back to take a look,
at what is written in Life's Book.
I see that those in fallen mind,
don't want me Love to ever find.

O Venus, show me how to serve,
your cosmic beauty I observe.
What love from Venus you now bring,
our planets do in tandem sing.

O Venus, service so divine,
you are for earth a cosmic sign.
Your selfless service is now mine,
a life in service I define.

2. They have perverted Love so much,
that true Love cannot people touch.
Their view of Love has such defect,
to true Love they cannot connect.

O Venus, your love is the key,
the hardened hearts on earth are free.
Embracing future bright and bold,
our planet's story is retold.

**O Venus, service so divine,
you are for earth a cosmic sign.
Your selfless service is now mine,
a life in service I define.**

3. O Venus, teach me Love to know,
Divine Love on me now bestow.
O teach me, Love's Ambassador,
for I am always wanting More.

O Venus, loving Mother mine,
my heart your love does now refine.
I am the open door for love,
descending like a Holy Dove.

**O Venus, service so divine,
you are for earth a cosmic sign.
Your selfless service is now mine,
a life in service I define.**

4. The fallen beings launched the plot,
that caused true Love to be forgot.
Through standard of duality,
insert conditionality.

O Venus, play the secret note,
that is for hatred antidote.
All poisoned hearts you gently heal,
as love's true story you reveal.

O Venus, service so divine,
you are for earth a cosmic sign.
Your selfless service is now mine,
a life in service I define.

5. And when conditions we define,
creating lie of "me" and "mine,"
the sacred line we sink below,
obstructing Love's eternal flow.

O Venus, love fills every need,
for truly, love is God's first seed.
O let it blossom, let it grow,
sweep earth into your loving flow.

O Venus, service so divine,
you are for earth a cosmic sign.
Your selfless service is now mine,
a life in service I define.

6. For Love does drive the universe,
it never goes into reverse.
True Love presents an "either-or,"
you either shrink or become More.

O Venus, music of the spheres,
heard by those who God reveres.
Our voices now as one we raise,
singing in adoring praise.

O Venus, service so divine,
you are for earth a cosmic sign.
Your selfless service is now mine,
a life in service I define.

7. When we depart from Love's own stream,
of ownership we might well dream.
The force of Kali will make sure,
that Babel's tower won't endure.

O Venus, we are joining ranks,
Sanat Kumara we give thanks.
Our planet has received new life,
to lift her out of war and strife.

O Venus, service so divine,
you are for earth a cosmic sign.
Your selfless service is now mine,
a life in service I define.

8. When mind is by conditions set,
it sees true Love as unfair threat.
Love's Ruby Ray soon will consume,
what traps you in a darkened room.

O Venus, your sweet melody,
consumes veil of duality.
Absorbed in tones of Cosmic Love,
all conflict we now rise above.

O Venus, service so divine,
you are for earth a cosmic sign.
Your selfless service is now mine,
a life in service I define.

9. For true Love will to set life free,
to flow with Love eternally.
And it is now my heart's desire,
to let Love take me ever higher.

O Venus, shining Morning Star,
a cosmic herald, that you are.
The earth set free by sacred sound,
our planet is now heaven-bound.

O Venus, service so divine,
you are for earth a cosmic sign.
Your selfless service is now mine,
a life in service I define.

3. I let go of all conditions

1. As my conditions I reject,
a greater Love I do detect.
O Venus, as we Love employ
I sing with you an ode to joy.

O Venus, show me how to serve,
your cosmic beauty I observe.
What love from Venus you now bring,
our planets do in tandem sing.

O Venus, service so divine,
you are for earth a cosmic sign.
Your selfless service is now mine,
a life in service I define.

2. As all conditions I let go,
I join with Venus in Love's flow.
I feel Love as a rushing stream,
awakens me from human dream.

O Venus, your love is the key,
the hardened hearts on earth are free.
Embracing future bright and bold,
our planet's story is retold.

O Venus, service so divine,
you are for earth a cosmic sign.
Your selfless service is now mine,
a life in service I define.

3. I see the world is just a stage,
my current role no more a cage.
My role conditions did define,
but I am free to change my mind.

O Venus, loving Mother mine,
my heart your love does now refine.
I am the open door for love,
descending like a Holy Dove.

O Venus, service so divine,
you are for earth a cosmic sign.
Your selfless service is now mine,
a life in service I define.

4. No matter what has gone before,
I hereby choose to become More.
Conditions I will simply lose,
as Love I consciously do choose.

O Venus, play the secret note,
that is for hatred antidote.
All poisoned hearts you gently heal,
as love's true story you reveal.

O Venus, service so divine,
you are for earth a cosmic sign.
Your selfless service is now mine,
a life in service I define.

5. To mission mine I am awake,
my place in cosmic plan I take.
Sanat Kumara, I will serve,
the victory you do deserve.

O Venus, love fills every need,
for truly, love is God's first seed.
O let it blossom, let it grow,
sweep earth into your loving flow.

O Venus, service so divine,
you are for earth a cosmic sign.
Your selfless service is now mine,
a life in service I define.

6. O Venus, loving Mother mine,
a higher service we define.
As I join in your loving song,
I am at home where I belong.

O Venus, music of the spheres,
heard by those who God reveres.
Our voices now as one we raise,
singing in adoring praise.

O Venus, service so divine,
you are for earth a cosmic sign.
Your selfless service is now mine,
a life in service I define.

7. My job on earth I do fulfill,
Love's power gives me diamond will.
All obstacles Love does consume,
my rightful role I do resume.

O Venus, we are joining ranks,
Sanat Kumara we give thanks.
Our planet has received new life,
to lift her out of war and strife.

O Venus, service so divine,
you are for earth a cosmic sign.
Your selfless service is now mine,
a life in service I define.

8. Sanat Kumara's rescue throng,
is truly where I do belong.
And thus the earth we will now lift,
by freely sharing Love's own gift.

O Venus, your sweet melody,
consumes veil of duality.
Absorbed in tones of Cosmic Love,
all conflict we now rise above.

O Venus, service so divine,
you are for earth a cosmic sign.
Your selfless service is now mine,
a life in service I define.

9. When no conditions I maintain,
nothing I do can be in vain.
Each sharing of the Sacred Love,
brings untold blessings from Above.

O Venus, shining Morning Star,
a cosmic herald, that you are.
The earth set free by sacred sound,
our planet is now heaven-bound.

O Venus, service so divine,
you are for earth a cosmic sign.
Your selfless service is now mine,
a life in service I define.

4. In Love I am free

1. O Love, what beauty in your eye,
O Love, conditions you defy.
O Love, all life you multiply,
O Love, for More I ever try.

O Venus, show me how to serve,
your cosmic beauty I observe.
What love from Venus you now bring,
our planets do in tandem sing.

O Venus, service so divine,
you are for earth a cosmic sign.
Your selfless service is now mine,
a life in service I define.

2. O Love, you are more than a dream,
O Love, an all-consuming stream.
O Love, I find true self-esteem,
O Love, my innocence redeem.

O Venus, your love is the key,
the hardened hearts on earth are free.
Embracing future bright and bold,
our planet's story is retold.

O Venus, service so divine,
you are for earth a cosmic sign.
Your selfless service is now mine,
a life in service I define.

3. O Love, you shatter darkest night,
O Love, you give me inner sight.
O Love, you burn forever bright,
O Love, you are my sacred right.

O Venus, loving Mother mine,
my heart your love does now refine.
I am the open door for love,
descending like a Holy Dove.

O Venus, service so divine,
you are for earth a cosmic sign.
Your selfless service is now mine,
a life in service I define.

4. O Love, you are a soundless sound,
O Love, the ego you confound.
O Love, my heart with you resound,
O Love, all people you astound.

O Venus, play the secret note,
that is for hatred antidote.
All poisoned hearts you gently heal,
as love's true story you reveal.

O Venus, service so divine,
you are for earth a cosmic sign.
Your selfless service is now mine,
a life in service I define.

5. O Love, my heart is now a prism,
O Love, for healing every schism.
O Love, you bring me optimism,
O Love, you are true realism.

O Venus, love fills every need,
for truly, love is God's first seed.
O let it blossom, let it grow,
sweep earth into your loving flow.

O Venus, service so divine,
you are for earth a cosmic sign.
Your selfless service is now mine,
a life in service I define.

6. O Love, a brand new paradigm,
O Love, your ladder I now climb.
O Love, you are my great pastime,
O Love, your beauty so sublime.

O Venus, music of the spheres,
heard by those who God reveres.
Our voices now as one we raise,
singing in adoring praise.

**O Venus, service so divine,
you are for earth a cosmic sign.
Your selfless service is now mine,
a life in service I define.**

7. O Love, you are eternal flow,
O Love, let Holy Spirit blow.
O Love, my heart is now aglow,
O Love, on all new life bestow.

O Venus, we are joining ranks,
Sanat Kumara we give thanks.
Our planet has received new life,
to lift her out of war and strife.

**O Venus, service so divine,
you are for earth a cosmic sign.
Your selfless service is now mine,
a life in service I define.**

8. O Love, you calm Samsara's Sea,
O Love, world peace you do decree.
O Love, with you I do agree,
O Love, in you I am carefree.

O Venus, your sweet melody,
consumes veil of duality.
Absorbed in tones of Cosmic Love,
all conflict we now rise above.

O Venus, service so divine,
you are for earth a cosmic sign.
Your selfless service is now mine,
a life in service I define.

9. O Love, release a healing shower,
O Love, show all their inner power.
O Love, this is the cosmic hour,
O Love, you do us all empower.

O Venus, shining Morning Star,
a cosmic herald, that you are.
The earth set free by sacred sound,
our planet is now heaven-bound.

O Venus, service so divine,
you are for earth a cosmic sign.
Your selfless service is now mine,
a life in service I define.

OM AH HUM,
VENUS GURU PADME SIDDHI HUM

(Chant 9X, 33X or more)

Sealing

In the name of the Divine Mother, I call to Lady Master Venus and Mother Mary for the sealing of myself and all people in my circle of influence in the creative flow of the Divine Mother, the River of Life. I call for the multiplication of my calls by all representatives of the Divine Mother, so that we form the perfect figure-eight flow of "As Above, so below." Thus, I accept that this is fully manifest, because the mouth of the Lord, the Divine Mother that I AM, has spoken it. Amen.

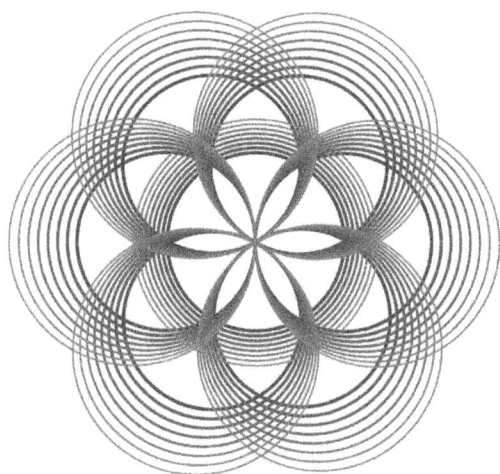

DECREE TO VENUS

In the name I AM THAT I AM, Jesus Christ, I call to all representatives of the Divine Mother, especially Lady Master Venus and Mother Mary, for the healing of my four lower bodies, especially for the transfiguration of my ability to accept unconditional love and let it flow through me. I call for the healing of all forms of conditional love, including...

[Make personal calls.]

1. O Venus, show me how to serve,
your cosmic beauty I observe.
What love from Venus you now bring,
our planets do in tandem sing.

**O Venus, service so divine,
you are for earth a cosmic sign.
Your selfless service is now mine,
a life in service I define.**

2. O Venus, your love is the key,
the hardened hearts on earth are free.
Embracing future bright and bold,
our planet's story is retold.

O Venus, service so divine,
you are for earth a cosmic sign.
Your selfless service is now mine,
a life in service I define.

3. O Venus, loving Mother mine,
my heart your love does now refine.
I am the open door for love,
descending like a Holy Dove.

O Venus, service so divine,
you are for earth a cosmic sign.
Your selfless service is now mine,
a life in service I define.

4. O Venus, play the secret note,
that is for hatred antidote.
All poisoned hearts you gently heal,
as love's true story you reveal.

O Venus, service so divine,
you are for earth a cosmic sign.
Your selfless service is now mine,
a life in service I define.

5. O Venus, love fills every need,
for truly, love is God's first seed.
O let it blossom, let it grow,
sweep earth into your loving flow.

O Venus, service so divine,
you are for earth a cosmic sign.
Your selfless service is now mine,
a life in service I define.

6. O Venus, music of the spheres,
heard by those who God reveres.
Our voices now as one we raise,
singing in adoring praise.

O Venus, service so divine,
you are for earth a cosmic sign.
Your selfless service is now mine,
a life in service I define.

7. O Venus, we are joining ranks,
Sanat Kumara we give thanks.
Our planet has received new life,
to lift her out of war and strife.

O Venus, service so divine,
you are for earth a cosmic sign.
Your selfless service is now mine,
a life in service I define.

8. O Venus, your sweet melody,
consumes veil of duality.
Absorbed in tones of Cosmic Love,
all conflict we now rise above.

**O Venus, service so divine,
you are for earth a cosmic sign.
Your selfless service is now mine,
a life in service I define.**

9. O Venus, shining Morning Star,
a cosmic herald, that you are.
The earth set free by sacred sound,
our planet is now heaven-bound.

**O Venus, service so divine,
you are for earth a cosmic sign.
Your selfless service is now mine,
a life in service I define.**

Sealing

In the name of the Divine Mother, I call to Lady Master Venus and Mother Mary for the sealing of myself and all people in my circle of influence in the creative flow of the Divine Mother, the River of Life. I call for the multiplication of my calls by all representatives of the Divine Mother, so that we form the perfect figure-eight flow of "As Above, so below." Thus, I accept that this is fully manifest, because the mouth of the Lord, the Divine Mother that I AM, has spoken it. Amen.

Song of Life 8

OMEGA FLOW

In the name I AM THAT I AM, Jesus Christ, I call to all representatives of the Divine Mother, especially Omega and Mother Mary, for the healing of my four lower bodies, especially for the transfiguration of my sense of identity so I can accept myself as part of the Divine Mother and have the perfect balance between masculine and feminine. I call for the healing of all imbalances, including…

[Make personal calls.]

> When Father-Mother are as One,
> I see the rising of the Son.
> My Christic balance is the key,
> extremes they cannot capture me.
>
> When I am centered in the One,
> my inner balance I have won.
> My I AM Presence now can do,
> all that it wants through Conscious You.
>
> When I have balanced Yang and Yin,
> the victory of Christ I win.
> As Mara's demons I transcend,
> the eightfold path I do ascend.

When I complete the sacred quest,
fulfilling every subtle test.
With Jesus I the ghost release,
Gautama Buddha shows me peace.

When with Maitreya I am free,
Sanat Kumara greeting me.
Alpha-Omega are now one,
I am with them in Central Sun.

When nexus of their figure-eight,
opens up the cosmic gate.
With my Creator I can be,
I AM in true polarity.

When I return to planet earth,
a brand new Self is given birth.
I know now what for all is best,
the Will of God is manifest.

1. I am in the Central Sun

1. In Central Sun's Assembly Hall,
I lift my eyes to pillars tall.
They are such awe-inspiring sight,
reminding me that all is light.

Omega, I now meditate,
upon your throne in cosmic gate.
I'm born out of the figure-eight,
that Alpha and you co-create.

O Song of Life, you vitalize,
all hearts you truly synchronize.
O Sacred Sound, you alchemize,
turn earth into a paradise.

2. And up above, expansive dome,
reminding me that this is home.
For this is where it all began,
the Flow of Life from God to man.

Omega, in your sacred space,
my cosmic parents I embrace.
I see that it is such a grace,
that I take part in cosmic race.

O Song of Life, you vitalize,
all hearts you truly synchronize.
O Sacred Sound, you alchemize,
turn earth into a paradise.

3. Alpha-Omega on their throne,
emitting life's most sacred tone.
It does secure the harmony
of all who sing life's melody.

Omega in the Central Sun,
you show me life is cosmic fun.
And thus a victory is won,
my homeward journey has begun.

O Song of Life, you vitalize,
all hearts you truly synchronize.
O Sacred Sound, you alchemize,
turn earth into a paradise.

4. Between them is the figure-eight,
the nexus is the cosmic gate.
Beyond it my Creator lives,
the one who self-awareness gives.

Omega, femininity
is doorway to infinity.
With you I have affinity,
to know my own divinity.

O Song of Life, you vitalize,
all hearts you truly synchronize.
O Sacred Sound, you alchemize,
turn earth into a paradise.

5. As into timeless space I gaze,
my heart resounds with grateful praise.
Upon the Cosmic Cube I sit,
my freeborn Self does light emit.

Omega, in your cosmic flow,
my plan divine I clearly know.
My heart is now a lamp aglow,
as love on all I do bestow.

O Song of Life, you vitalize,
all hearts you truly synchronize.
O Sacred Sound, you alchemize,
turn earth into a paradise.

6. The work of God my Self reveres,
I hear the Music of the Spheres.
I see that light will oscillate,
in sync with sound I propagate.

Omega, cosmic Mother Flame,
this is the light from which I came.
As I take part in cosmic game,
Christ victory I do proclaim.

O Song of Life, you vitalize,
all hearts you truly synchronize.
O Sacred Sound, you alchemize,
turn earth into a paradise.

7. I feel the urge within my heart,
to be of Cosmic Dance a part.
My sense of self I wish to grow,
as God breathes out, I join the flow.

Omega, I now comprehend,
why I did to earth descend.
And thus I fully do intend,
to help this planet to ascend.

**O Song of Life, you vitalize,
all hearts you truly synchronize.
O Sacred Sound, you alchemize,
turn earth into a paradise.**

8. The World of Form before me lies,
I look beneath the lofty skies.
My eyes fall on this planet earth,
and this is where I seek new birth.

Omega, I do now aspire,
to join the ranks of cosmic choir.
My heart burns with a Christic fire,
that is this planet's sanctifier.

**O Song of Life, you vitalize,
all hearts you truly synchronize.
O Sacred Sound, you alchemize,
turn earth into a paradise.**

9. I wish to bring a Spirit Spark,
to planet that is yet so dark.
And as my Spirit I extend,
I hope to help the earth ascend.

Omega, my heart is ablaze,
my life is in an upward phase.
Come teach me now the secret phrase,
so that I can this planet raise.

O Song of Life, you vitalize,
all hearts you truly synchronize.
O Sacred Sound, you alchemize,
turn earth into a paradise.

2. I claim my right to be on earth

1. As I am born in body dense,
the contrast is just so immense.
Yet I will give it my best try,
the light of God to multiply.

Omega, I now meditate,
upon your throne in cosmic gate.
I'm born out of the figure-eight,
that Alpha and you co-create.

O Song of Life, you vitalize,
all hearts you truly synchronize.
O Sacred Sound, you alchemize,
turn earth into a paradise.

2. Yet pretty soon I do detect,
that people will the light reject.
And this is truly quite a shock,
why do they me and God's light mock?

Omega, in your sacred space,
my cosmic parents I embrace.
I see that it is such a grace,
that I take part in cosmic race.

**O Song of Life, you vitalize,
all hearts you truly synchronize.
O Sacred Sound, you alchemize,
turn earth into a paradise.**

3. They say I do not have the right,
to be on earth and bring God's light.
They say this is a world apart,
I cannot be of God a part.

Omega in the Central Sun,
you show me life is cosmic fun.
And thus a victory is won,
my homeward journey has begun.

**O Song of Life, you vitalize,
all hearts you truly synchronize.
O Sacred Sound, you alchemize,
turn earth into a paradise.**

4. They say the earth is devil's lair,
I feel a sense of deep despair.
They say my Spirit must adapt,
for on this planet I am trapped.

Omega, femininity
is doorway to infinity.
With you I have affinity,
to know my own divinity.

**O Song of Life, you vitalize,
all hearts you truly synchronize.
O Sacred Sound, you alchemize,
turn earth into a paradise.**

5. Their condemnation so intense,
it truly shakes my confidence.
I start to think they might be right,
I start to see with dual sight.

Omega, in your cosmic flow,
my plan divine I clearly know.
My heart is now a lamp aglow,
as love on all I do bestow.

**O Song of Life, you vitalize,
all hearts you truly synchronize.
O Sacred Sound, you alchemize,
turn earth into a paradise.**

6. As they expose me to attack,
I one day start to fight them back.
And so it is a sad old fact,
to serpent's lie I did react.

Omega, cosmic Mother Flame,
this is the light from which I came.
As I take part in cosmic game,
Christ victory I do proclaim.

**O Song of Life, you vitalize,
all hearts you truly synchronize.
O Sacred Sound, you alchemize,
turn earth into a paradise.**

7. I start to think I came to fight,
the forces that uphold the night.
As good and evil I define,
I think the victory is mine.

Omega, I now comprehend,
why I did to earth descend.
And thus I fully do intend,
to help this planet to ascend.

**O Song of Life, you vitalize,
all hearts you truly synchronize.
O Sacred Sound, you alchemize,
turn earth into a paradise.**

8. Yet after fighting long and hard,
the fighting spirit I discard.
My mind is weary of the chore,
my heart cries out: There must be More.

Omega, I do now aspire,
to join the ranks of cosmic choir.
My heart burns with a Christic fire,
that is this planet's sanctifier.

O Song of Life, you vitalize,
all hearts you truly synchronize.
O Sacred Sound, you alchemize,
turn earth into a paradise.

9. As I cry out, the Christ I see,
breathing new life into me.
And as I leave behind each net,
on higher goal my mind is set.

Omega, my heart is ablaze,
my life is in an upward phase.
Come teach me now the secret phrase,
so that I can this planet raise.

O Song of Life, you vitalize,
all hearts you truly synchronize.
O Sacred Sound, you alchemize,
turn earth into a paradise.

3. I claim my divine identity

1. With Christ exposing serpent's lie,
the fallen standard I defy.
My Spirit will no more conform,
to fallen beings and their norm.

Omega, I now meditate,
upon your throne in cosmic gate.
I'm born out of the figure-eight,
that Alpha and you co-create.

O Song of Life, you vitalize,
all hearts you truly synchronize.
O Sacred Sound, you alchemize,
turn earth into a paradise.

2. Their darkness is but a mirage,
their posturing all camouflage.
As Christ in me is given birth,
I claim my right to be on earth.

Omega, in your sacred space,
my cosmic parents I embrace.
I see that it is such a grace,
that I take part in cosmic race.

O Song of Life, you vitalize,
all hearts you truly synchronize.
O Sacred Sound, you alchemize,
turn earth into a paradise.

3. With Christ I see reality,
that Mother's not my enemy.
With Mother I am now at peace,
as spirits old I do release.

Omega in the Central Sun,
you show me life is cosmic fun.
And thus a victory is won,
my homeward journey has begun.

O Song of Life, you vitalize,
all hearts you truly synchronize.
O Sacred Sound, you alchemize,
turn earth into a paradise.

4. I now accept my perfect right,
to raise the earth into the light.
In knowing Mother is the key,
I accept my femininity.

Omega, femininity
is doorway to infinity.
With you I have affinity,
to know my own divinity.

O Song of Life, you vitalize,
all hearts you truly synchronize.
O Sacred Sound, you alchemize,
turn earth into a paradise.

5. As I draw close to Mother's heart,
of Mother I am now a part.
In out-breath I with Father flow,
in in-breath I in Mother grow.

Omega, in your cosmic flow,
my plan divine I clearly know.
My heart is now a lamp aglow,
as love on all I do bestow.

O Song of Life, you vitalize,
all hearts you truly synchronize.
O Sacred Sound, you alchemize,
turn earth into a paradise.

6. The Ma-ter light I seek to raise,
a trail for all I hereby blaze.
For raising Mother is the key
to Spirit's sacred alchemy.

Omega, Cosmic Mother Flame,
this is the light from which I came.
As I take part in cosmic game,
Christ victory I do proclaim.

O Song of Life, you vitalize,
all hearts you truly synchronize.
O Sacred Sound, you alchemize,
turn earth into a paradise.

7. A flawless diamond is my mind,
in clarity the truth I find,
that I am Mother here below,
the Mind of God can through me flow.

Omega, I now comprehend,
why I did to earth descend.
And thus I fully do intend,
to help this planet to ascend.

O Song of Life, you vitalize,
all hearts you truly synchronize.
O Sacred Sound, you alchemize,
turn earth into a paradise.

8. When I accept my Mother role,
no one on earth can me control.
My I AM Presence is the force,
that sets my life on upward course.

Omega, I do now aspire,
to join the ranks of cosmic choir.
My heart burns with a Christic fire,
that is this planet's sanctifier.

O Song of Life, you vitalize,
all hearts you truly synchronize.
O Sacred Sound, you alchemize,
turn earth into a paradise.

9. Accepting femininity,
is key to masculinity.
Omega in the Central Sun,
with Father-Mother I am one.

Omega, my heart is ablaze,
my life is in an upward phase.
Come teach me now the secret phrase,
so that I can this planet raise.

O Song of Life, you vitalize,
all hearts you truly synchronize.
O Sacred Sound, you alchemize,
turn earth into a paradise.

4. I am the Divine Mother

1. I AM Omega here below,
God Power I on all bestow.
Creator mine forever One,
Christ victory already won.

Omega, I now meditate,
upon your throne in cosmic gate.
I'm born out of the figure-eight,
that Alpha and you co-create.

O Song of Life, you vitalize,
all hearts you truly synchronize.
O Sacred Sound, you alchemize,
turn earth into a paradise.

2. I AM Omega here below,
God Wisdom I on all bestow.
Alpha-Omega makes it two,
as balance always I pursue.

Omega, in your sacred space,
my cosmic parents I embrace.
I see that it is such a grace,
that I take part in cosmic race.

**O Song of Life, you vitalize,
all hearts you truly synchronize.
O Sacred Sound, you alchemize,
turn earth into a paradise.**

3. I AM Omega here below,
God Love on all I do bestow.
The firstborn Son now makes it three,
and I give birth to Christ in me.

Omega in the Central Sun,
you show me life is cosmic fun.
And thus a victory is won,
my homeward journey has begun.

**O Song of Life, you vitalize,
all hearts you truly synchronize.
O Sacred Sound, you alchemize,
turn earth into a paradise.**

4. I AM Omega here below,
God Purity I do bestow.
With Holy Spirit it is four,
and I am now becoming More.

Omega, femininity
is doorway to infinity.
With you I have affinity,
to know my own divinity.

O Song of Life, you vitalize,
all hearts you truly synchronize.
O Sacred Sound, you alchemize,
turn earth into a paradise.

5. I AM Omega here below,
God Vision I on all bestow.
The Sacred Feminine is five,
I am so glad to be alive.

Omega, in your cosmic flow,
my plan divine I clearly know.
My heart is now a lamp aglow,
as love on all I do bestow.

O Song of Life, you vitalize,
all hearts you truly synchronize.
O Sacred Sound, you alchemize,
turn earth into a paradise.

6. I AM Omega here below,
God Peace on all I do bestow.
In symmetry there is now six,
I now transcend the crucifix.

Omega, cosmic Mother Flame,
this is the light from which I came.
As I take part in cosmic game,
Christ victory I do proclaim.

O Song of Life, you vitalize,
all hearts you truly synchronize.
O Sacred Sound, you alchemize,
turn earth into a paradise.

7. I AM Omega here below,
God Freedom I on all bestow.
In unity of sacred seven,
I am ascending into heaven.

Omega, I now comprehend,
why I did to earth descend.
And thus I fully do intend,
to help this planet to ascend.

O Song of Life, you vitalize,
all hearts you truly synchronize.
O Sacred Sound, you alchemize,
turn earth into a paradise.

8. I AM Omega here below,
the Middle Way I do bestow.
With Buddha and the Path of Eight,
all people we illuminate.

Omega, I do now aspire,
to join the ranks of cosmic choir.
My heart burns with a Christic fire,
that is this planet's sanctifier.

O Song of Life, you vitalize,
all hearts you truly synchronize.
O Sacred Sound, you alchemize,
turn earth into a paradise.

9. I AM Omega here below,
acceleration I bestow.
Accelerate by nine times nine,
our planet truly is Divine.

Omega, my heart is ablaze,
my life is in an upward phase.
Come teach me now the secret phrase,
so that I can this planet raise.

O Song of Life, you vitalize,
all hearts you truly synchronize.
O Sacred Sound, you alchemize,
turn earth into a paradise.

I AM ALPHA AND OMEGA,
IN THE FIGURE-EIGHT OF BEING

(Chant 9X, 33X or more)

Sealing

In the name of the Divine Mother, I call to Omega and Mother Mary for the sealing of myself and all people in my circle of influence in the creative flow of the Divine Mother, the River of Life. I call for the multiplication of my calls by all representatives of the Divine Mother, so that we form the perfect figure-eight flow of "As Above, so below." Thus, I accept that this is fully manifest, because the mouth of the Lord, the Divine Mother that I AM, has spoken it. Amen.

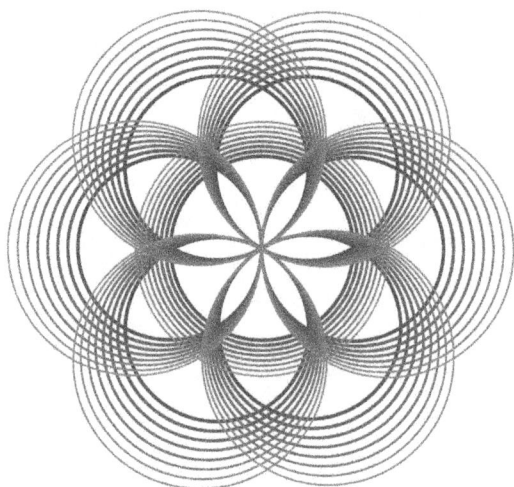

DECREE TO OMEGA

In the name I AM THAT I AM, Jesus Christ, I call to all representatives of the Divine Mother, especially Omega and Mother Mary, for the healing of my four lower bodies, especially for the transfiguration of my sense of identity so I can accept myself as part of the Divine Mother and have the perfect balance between masculine and feminine. I call for the healing of all imbalances, including...

[Make personal calls.]

1. Omega, I now meditate,
upon your throne in cosmic gate.
I'm born out of the figure-eight,
that Alpha and you co-create.

**O Song of Life, you vitalize,
all hearts you truly synchronize.
O Sacred Sound, you alchemize,
turn earth into a paradise.**

2. Omega, in your sacred space,
my cosmic parents I embrace.
I see that it is such a grace,
that I take part in cosmic race.

O Song of Life, you vitalize,
all hearts you truly synchronize.
O Sacred Sound, you alchemize,
turn earth into a paradise.

3. Omega in the Central Sun,
you show me life is cosmic fun.
And thus a victory is won,
my homeward journey has begun.

O Song of Life, you vitalize,
all hearts you truly synchronize.
O Sacred Sound, you alchemize,
turn earth into a paradise.

4. Omega, femininity
is doorway to infinity.
With you I have affinity,
to know my own divinity.

O Song of Life, you vitalize,
all hearts you truly synchronize.
O Sacred Sound, you alchemize,
turn earth into a paradise.

5. Omega, in your cosmic flow,
my plan divine I clearly know.
My heart is now a lamp aglow,
as love on all I do bestow.

O Song of Life, you vitalize,
all hearts you truly synchronize.
O Sacred Sound, you alchemize,
turn earth into a paradise.

6. Omega, cosmic Mother Flame,
this is the light from which I came.
As I take part in cosmic game,
Christ victory I do proclaim.

O Song of Life, you vitalize,
all hearts you truly synchronize.
O Sacred Sound, you alchemize,
turn earth into a paradise.

7. Omega, I now comprehend,
why I did to earth descend.
And thus I fully do intend,
to help this planet to ascend.

O Song of Life, you vitalize,
all hearts you truly synchronize.
O Sacred Sound, you alchemize,
turn earth into a paradise.

8. Omega, I do now aspire,
to join the ranks of cosmic choir.
My heart burns with a Christic fire,
that is this planet's sanctifier.

O Song of Life, you vitalize,
all hearts you truly synchronize.
O Sacred Sound, you alchemize,
turn earth into a paradise.

9. Omega, my heart is ablaze,
my life is in an upward phase.
Come teach me now the secret phrase,
so that I can this planet raise.

O Song of Life, you vitalize,
all hearts you truly synchronize.
O Sacred Sound, you alchemize,
turn earth into a paradise.

Sealing

In the name of the Divine Mother, I call to Omega and Mother Mary for the sealing of myself and all people in my circle of influence in the creative flow of the Divine Mother, the River of Life. I call for the multiplication of my calls by all representatives of the Divine Mother, so that we form the perfect figure-eight flow of "As Above, so below." Thus, I accept that this is fully manifest, because the mouth of the Lord, the Divine Mother that I AM, has spoken it. Amen.

GENERAL SEALING

In the name of the Divine Mother, I call to Maraytaii, Nada, Kuan Yin, Mother Mary, Portia, Liberty, Venus and Omega for the sealing of myself and all people in my circle of influence in the creative flow of the Divine Mother, the River of Life. I call for the multiplication of my calls by all representatives of the Divine Mother, so that we form the perfect figure-eight flow of "As Above, so below." Thus, I accept that this is fully manifest, because the mouth of the Lord, the Divine Mother that I AM, has spoken it. Amen.

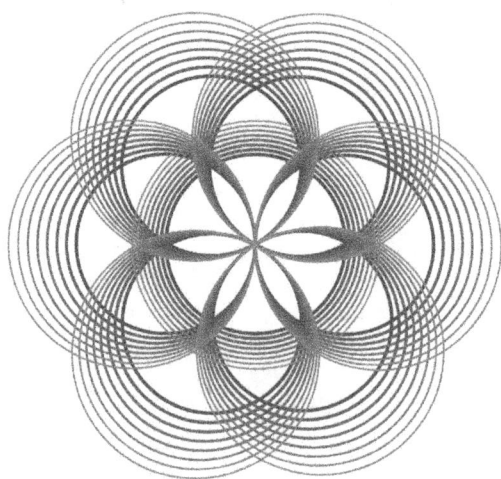

GLOSSARY

AKASHA

An energy of a higher vibration than anything else in the material realm. It serves as a recording device, recording everything that has ever happened in the material world. People with developed faculties can read the Akashic records. In the future, it will be possible to read them with technological devices.

ALCHMY

In popular belief, the process of transforming base metals into gold. The deeper, mystical meaning is the transformation of the base human consciousness into the gold of a more spiritualized awareness, such as Christ consciousness.

ALPHA AND OMEGA

Two spiritual beings who reside in the central sun, the highest level of the world of form.

ANGEL

A self-aware being that is not created to take physical embodiment. Angels serve in a variety of capacities, the most commonly known for us is as messengers who deliver a message from the spiritual realm to human beings. Another important function is angels who protect us against lower energies or dark forces.

ANTI-CHRIST

The consciousness of separation and duality. This consciousness forms a filter that distorts perception in such a way, that it seems plausible that we are separate beings, separated from God, from each other and from the material universe. The more firmly beings are trapped in this consciousness, the more real the illusion of separation seems to them. Thus, they will be acting as if they truly are separate beings, meaning they will believe that what they do to others will not affect themselves. This is the origin of man's inhumanity to man and the origin of evil. Human beings can be trapped in this consciousness, but so can non-material beings, forming the dark forces.

ARCHANGEL, ARCHEIA

Angels are organized into bands, and each band is led by an archangel. Each archangel has a feminine complement, called an archeia. There is such a pair for each of the seven rays, but there are also other bands of angels.

ASCENDED MASTER

Normally refers to a being who was embodied as a human being on earth and who, often after many embodiments, qualified for the process of the ascension. The term can also be used more broadly to refer to all beings in the spiritual realm, even those who have not taken embodiment in the material world.

ASCENSION

A process whereby a being evolves to the self-awareness represented by the full Christ consciousness. In this state of consciousness, one can see through all of the lies created by the illusion of separation and duality. Thus, one sees the underlying reality that nothing can be separated from the Creator and that all self-aware beings are extensions of the Creator. One therefore seeks to raise all life, instead of seeking to raise oneself as a separate being. After a being ascends, it resides permanently in the spiritual realm and does not have to reembody.

ASTRAL PLANE

Everything is made from energy, and energy is a continuum of vibrations. There are certain divisions of this energy continuum, for example the material universe is made from vibrations within a certain spectrum. Yet the material universe has four divisions: the etheric (identity) level, the mental level, the emotional level and the physical level.

The emotional level itself has further divisions, and the lowest of these are created when people engage in negative emotions, such as fear, anger and hatred. The astral plane is a division within the emotional realm, and it resembles the visions of hell that people have had throughout the ages.

ATLANTIS

A previous civilization that inhabited a continent in the mid Atlantic. This continent disappeared around 10,000 years ago due to the actions of the inhabitants. The atlantean civilization was technologically superior to our time, but due to the lack of spiritual awareness, the inhabitants caused the civilization to self-destruct due to a misqualification of energy, which led to warfare and cataclysm.

AQUARIAN AGE

There is a precession of astrological cycles, lasting approximately 2,150 years each. The previous age was the Age of Pisces, for which Jesus was the spiritual master. For the Aquarian age, the ascended master Saint Germain is the master. According to Saint Germain, the Aquarian age was officially inaugurated on March 22, 2010.

AURA

An energy field surrounding the human body. There are levels of the aura, corresponding to the levels of the material realm. You have an identity body, a mental body and an emotional body beyond the physical body.

CARNAL MIND

Sometimes used by ascended masters to refer to the entire lower consciousness, including the ego. Can also be used more specifically to refer to that part of the subconscious mind, which is designed to take care of the functions of the physical body. This includes certain basic instincts, such as protection, food and propagation. The carnal mind will seek to satisfy these needs without any regard for long-term interests and thus needs to be under the control of your conscious mind.

CAUSAL BODY

An energy "body" surrounding your I AM Presence. It stores all of the attainment gained and the lessons learned from all of your embodiments. When you raise your consciousness sufficiently, you can make use of this attainment for fulfilling your divine plan.

CATCH-22

Described by the popular saying "you can't get there from here." It is a seemingly impossible situation that you cannot get out of. The ascended masters use this to refer to the mechanisms created through the illusion of separation and duality. The mind of anti-christ creates innumerable catch-22s in order to stop or slow down our spiritual growth. They are always based on an illusion, which means you can transcend them by changing your perspective. Note that a catch-22 often appears as a problem that you have to solve. Yet the problem has no solution, so the real solution is to walk away from the struggle.

CHAKRA

A focal point within your aura. There are seven major chakras, corresponding to each of the seven spiritual rays. If your chakras are pure, high-frequency energy from your I AM Presence can stream through them, and this gives you maximum creative powers. If your chakras are polluted, the stream of higher energies is reduced, and instead the chakras can become open doors for lower energies to enter your aura. Severely polluted chakras can open you to energies from the astral plane.

CHELA, CHELASHIP

A Sanskrit word that is often translated as "slave." This refers to Indian spiritual tradition, where a person makes him- or herself the virtual slave of a spiritual teacher, or guru, who will thereby expose the student's ego. Used by the ascended masters to refer to a sincere student, who is willing to submit to the disciplines of the spiritual path, designed to expose the ego.

CHOHAN

For each of the seven spiritual rays, there is an ascended master who serves as the leader or main teacher. This spiritual office is called the "chohan."

CHRIST

In its broadest sense, this refers to the basic consciousness out of which everything in the world of form is created. The purpose is to maintain the oneness between the Creator and its creation. This is especially relevant for beings with free will, who have the option to descend into the illusion of separation, thereby believing they are separated from their source. The Christ consciousness ensures that no matter how far you descend into separation, you always have the option to return to oneness with the Creator. Because the Christ consciousness is within everything that is created, you can never go to a place where you are unreachable for Christ.

In a more specific sense, Christ refers to a being who has overcome the illusion of separation and has attained the Christ consciousness. There are degrees of Christ consciousness.

CHRIST SELF

A mediator sent by ascended masters to assist beings who have become trapped in separation and duality. Most people know their Christ selves as intuition or the "still, small voice within." The Christ self does not actually tell you what choices to make. It seeks to give you a frame of reference for making better choices. The Christ self will not necessarily give you an ultimate or absolute truth. It will give you an insight that is a bit higher than your present state of consciousness.

CHRIST DISCERNMENT

The ability to see through the innumerable illusions created through the consciousness of separation and duality. Also the ability to see the underlying oneness behind all visible phenomena.

CHRISTHOOD

When a being has attained the Christ consciousness, that being is said to have put on Christhood.

CONSCIOUS YOU

The core of your lower being. It is the Conscious You that descends from the spiritual realm as an extension of your I AM Presence. It is the conscious you that is the seat of your free will. However, you make choices based on the perception you have. It is possible for the Conscious You to have pure perception, which means it serves as an open door for the I AM Presence. However, when beings go into separation the Conscious You projects itself into an outer self or role, and it now perceives everything through the filter of that separate self. Thus, it will often make choices as if it really were a separate being.

The important point is that the Conscious You is and will always remain pure awareness. This means that while the Conscious You can project itself into any role it chooses, it can never lose the ability to extricate itself from that role and attain the Christ consciousness in which it can say with Jesus: "I and my father (my I AM Presence) are one."

COSMIC BEING

A spiritual being who holds a specific spiritual office, usually a focus of a certain divine quality. Cosmic beings have never taken embodiment on earth as they ascended in a higher sphere.

CREATOR

The being who created the particular world of form in which we exist. There are other worlds of forms created by other Creators. A Creator must create a world of form out of its own Being, meaning the Creator experiences everything that happens in a given world.

DARK FORCES

Beings who have become trapped in the illusion of separation and duality. Many such beings reside in the astral plane. Everything in the material universe is sustained by a stream of energy from a higher realm. Yet when you begin to deliberately harm other self-aware beings, you are cut off from receiving energy from a higher realm. Thus, you can sustain an existence only by stealing energy from beings in the material realm. This means that dark forces can continue to exist only by stealing energy from humans, and they do this by getting us to misqualify energy through lower emotions and selfish acts.

Dark forces can take over the minds of human beings (if people let them), and most of the warfare and crime seen on earth is caused by dark forces. They do this by agitating people to violate others, and the pain caused releases energy that the dark forces can use to sustain themselves.

DECREE

A spiritual technique for invoking high-frequency energy from the spiritual realm and directing it into specific conditions on the personal or planetary level. A decree is a worded expression, usually in rhyme, that is spoken aloud with great power and authority.

DHARMA

In Buddhist tradition, the sacred work that you came here to do. Also refers to your divine plan, which is the positive qualities you wanted to bring to earth before deciding to take embodiment here.

DIVINE MOTHER

A spiritual office that represents the feminine aspect of God to planet earth. Currently, this office is held by the ascended master Mother Mary.

DIVINE DIRECTION

Guidance that you receive from a higher source through your Christ self. The guidance can be from your I AM Presence, an ascended master or the cosmic being known as the Great Divine Director, who represents divine direction.

DIVINE PLAN

A plan for what you want to accomplish in this embodiment. This includes the spiritual gift you want to bring to earth, experiences you want to have, lessons you want to learn and karma you want to balance. Often, this means there are certain people you want to meet and with whom you want to engage in various types of relationships.

DUALITY, DUALITY CONSCIOUSNESS

When the Conscious You sees with pure perception, it sees the underlying reality that all life is one and came from the same source. The duality consciousness obscures this oneness, and it makes it seem like matter is separated from spirit, humans are separated from God and people are separated from each other.

Duality also implies a negative polarity between two opposites that work against each other, one seeking to annihilate the other. Thus, duality always involves two opposing sides, and there is usually a value judgment attached to them, making one good and the other evil.

Duality is always an illusion, because nothing can change or destroy the oneness of all life. Thus, duality can exist only as an illusion in the minds of self-aware beings. As long as you are blinded by duality, you cannot attain Christ consciousness and thus cannot ascend.

Glossary

EIGHTFOLD PATH OF THE BUDDHA

Traditionally, the path prescribed by Gautama Buddha for overcoming suffering. However, a deeper mystical understanding is that it represents the path of mastering the first seven spiritual rays and the eighth ray of integration.

ELEMENTALS

The world of form is created through a hierarchy of beings that extend from the Creator. For example, planet earth was created by seven beings in the spiritual realm, called the Elohim. They envisioned the blueprint for the earth and projected it into the four levels of the material realm.

However, the blueprint is brought into physical manifestation by four classes of elemental beings. These are beings that have a lower self-awareness than humans, but who can grow by serving to help build the material world. The elementals in the four realms are named as follows:
-Etheric realm, fire elementals or salamanders
-Mental realm, air elementals or sylphs
-Emotional realm, water elementals or undines
-Physical realm, earth elementals or gnomes.

ELOHIM

Ascended beings with such a high level of consciousness that they have complete mastery over the creation of matter. There is a masculine/feminine polarity of Elohim for each of the seven rays.

EMOTIONAL BODY

An aspect of your aura/mind that houses your emotional energies.

ETHERIC BODY

An aspect of your aura/mind that houses your sense of identity.

EVIL, THE VEIL OF MAYA

In Buddhist tradition, the veil of Maya is what obscures reality to beings in embodiment. This reality is that everything is the Buddha nature, in other words that all life is one. This veil is actually created because the matter universe is made from energy of a certain density, which makes it impossible for the physical senses to detect that even matter is made from spiritual light. Thus, this energy veil is abbreviated as evil.

FALL

In its broadest sense, the term refers to the process whereby a self-aware being descends into the consciousness of separation. Before the fall, you will see yourself as a being who is not isolated but is connected to something greater than yourself. After the fall, you will be convinced that you are a separate being, who has been abandoned or punished by God.

The important distinction is that after the fall, you will find it difficult to take responsibility for your own growth. Because the fall was caused by your own choices, it can only be undone through your own choices. Yet when you think you are a separate being, you think you can do whatever you want without considering the consequences for others. This causes you to engage in an ongoing struggle against other people, which can lead to a state of mind where you think you have to fight against other people, the matter universe or even God.

This state of mind becomes a catch-22, because as long as you will not accept that you have created your own situation as a result of your own choices, you cannot change those choices. Instead, you are seeking to create a change in your situation by forcing other people, the matter world or even God to come under your control. You are seeking to change the splinter in the eyes of others while ignoring the beam in your own eye.

FALLEN BEINGS OR FALLEN ANGELS

In its broadest sense, refers to all beings who are blinded by the duality consciousness. Yet the masters often use this more specifically to refer to a group of beings who fell in a previous sphere. The important distinction is that these beings had attained considerable attainment before they fell, which means they are often superior to the beings who started their existence in this world.

In world history, fallen beings have often become powerful but abusive leaders, and obvious examples are Hitler, Stalin and Mao. Yet many fallen beings hold important positions without visibly abusing their power and thus have a huge influence in society. Their main characteristic is that they are absolutely sure that they are right because they feel they are superior to most people on earth. There are also fallen beings who are not in physical embodiment, but who reside in the astral plane or the mental realm.

FALLEN CONSCIOUSNESS

The consciousness of the fallen beings. In its broadest sense, the illusion of separation and duality. It can also refer more specifically to the consciousness of feeling superior to others, wanting to have special privileges or wanting others to follow you.

The main characteristic of the fallen consciousness is the belief that the ends can justify the means. This often causes people to believe they are engaged in an epic struggle and that it is their duty to use all means available to eradicate what they have defined as evil. Thus, the underlying belief is that you have the right to define what is good and evil, because you have a godlike status.

FOUR LEVELS OF THE MATERIAL REALM

Everything is made from energy, so the entire world of form is made from energies of various vibrational qualities. There is a continuum of vibrations, ranging from the highest level, the level of the Creator, to the lowest. In between one can define several divisions, compartments or octaves of vibrations. For example, one major division is between the spiritual realm and the material realm.

There are several divisions in the spiritual realm, whereas in the material realm there are four divisions. They are, from higher to lower vibrations:
-the etheric or identity level
-the mental level
-the emotional level
-the physical level

FOHAT

Refers to written or spoken word that is inspired from a higher source and endowed with spiritual light. Words become cups or chalices that carry spiritual light.

FOUR LOWER BODIES, FOUR LEVELS OF THE MIND

Corresponding to the four levels of the material universe, the masters sometimes say that we humans have four lower bodies, the identity body, the mental body, the emotional body and the physical body.

The masters also talk about four levels of the mind, where the identity mind houses our deepest sense of identity (who we are and what we can do), the mental mind houses our thoughts (how we can do things), the emotional mind houses our feelings (why we want to/ have to do something) and the physical mind relates to the needs of the body.

FREE WILL

The masters teach that it is extremely important to understand free will, especially in relation to the duality consciousness. Free will is the basic law that guides the function of the material realm. For example, the earth was created by the Elohim in a much higher state than what we see today. There was originally no lack of resources, no imbalances in nature and no diseases.

These limiting conditions have been created because a majority of human beings used their free will to descend into duality. Nature – meaning the elemental beings – had no choice but to outpicture as material conditions what was in the consciousness of a majority of the people. Human beings were created to have dominion over the earth, and the elemental beings can only take on the images we hold in our identity, mental, emotional and physical minds.

Yet the important point about free will is that we have the right to, at any time, transcend our previous choices. God and the ascended masters will never seek to stop us from transcending previous choices. It is only the ego and the dark forces who will seek to make us believe we are bound by past choices.

GURU

A Sanskrit word for teacher or master.

GARDEN OF EDEN

The deeper symbolism behind the Biblical concept of the Garden of Eden is that it represents a schoolroom in which self-aware beings are being prepared to take embodiment on earth. The "God" mentioned in the Bible was the ascended master Lord Maitreya, who was the "headmaster" of the mystery school.

Students were given graded lessons, and only more advanced students were meant to take the lesson represented by the duality consciousness. However, there was a number of beings in the mystery school, who had fallen in a previous sphere. These beings are symbolized by the Serpent, and they deceived some students into taking the initiation of duality before they were prepared by the teacher. This initiation is symbolized by the "fruit of the knowledge of good and evil," which makes beings think they are like gods and can define what is good and evil without the Christ consciousness.

The symbolism is that the fallen beings have deceived most people on earth into believing in the dualistic lies. This is what causes all conflict and struggle on earth. The only solution is that a critical mass of people follow the true path of initiation and attain Christ consciousness. The real purpose of the ascended masters is to help us do this.

GOD, FOUR ASPECTS OF GOD

In mystical teachings, the world is seen as being made from one underlying element, called ether, which manifests as the four elements of fire, air, water and earth. One can likewise look at five aspects of God. The ether element corresponds to the original or undifferentiated Creator, which has not yet expressed itself in the world of form. As the Creator begins to express itself, it manifests itself as four aspects:

Father, meaning the outgoing force, the will to create. For us, the ascended masters represent the father element, yet we also represent the father element on earth.

Mother, meaning the contracting or balancing force. Compared to the Creator, everything in the world of form is the Mother. So we humans are part of the Divine Mother. Yet when we co-create by superimposing mental images upon the Ma-ter light, then this mother light represents mother for us.

Son or Christ, meaning the consciousness that unifies the Creator (who is beyond form) with everything that has form. It is also the element that separates the real from the unreal by seeing through all dualistic illusions.

Holy Spirit, means the force that drives all self-aware beings to return to their source. Since the beginning of the world of form, innumerable beings have gone through the process of the ascension and this has created a force or momentum that makes up the Holy Spirit.

GOD FLAME

Your true individuality is not what we normally call your personality; it is anchored in your I AM Presence. Because your I AM Presence is made from energies of a higher vibration than anything in the material universe, it appears as a flame. Thus, your true individuality is sometimes referred to as your God flame.

GOLDEN AGE

At present, the earth is in a lower state than originally intended. This is caused by a majority of people being deceived by the duality consciousness, which inevitably leads to various conflicts and limitations. Yet the goal of the ascended masters, especially Saint Germain as the leader of the coming 2,000 year cycle, is to inspire a critical mass of people to walk the path of individual Christhood. As enough people raise their consciousness, society will begin to outpicture a much higher state than today, and this is commonly referred to as a Golden Age.

GREAT WHITE BROTHERHOOD

Another name for all ascended beings. The term "white" does not refer to race, but to the fact that ascended masters radiate a white light.

HATRED OF THE MOTHER

The Ma-ter light forms the feminine polarity to the Creator. It allows us to project any mental image upon it we want, and then it faithfully reflects back to us physical circumstances that reflect the images in our consciousness. When people enter the fallen consciousness, they cannot take responsibility for themselves, meaning they will not recognize that the Mother can only reflect back what we project upon it and is not seeking to punish us. Instead, such beings feel like victims, and they do feel like matter, the Mother element, is seeking to punish them or prevent them from doing what they want. Thus, they can develop hatred of the mother. Yet since we are all part of the mother aspect of God, hatred of the Mother is a form of self-hatred.

HUMAN EGO

An element in the psyche that is created when the Conscious You descends into the illusion of separation and duality. The Conscious You is pure awareness, so it simply cannot act as a separate being. Yet it can step into a separate sense of self, and when it perceives the world through the perception filter of that self, it can believe that it really is a separate being. What makes this distorted perception seem real is the ego.

HUMAN CONSCIOUSNESS

In a general way, this refers to the consciousness that is currently considered normal for human beings. It can also be used more specifically to refer to the ego and the carnal mind.

I AM PRESENCE

Your higher or spiritual self. The Conscious You is an extension of your I AM Presence, and your highest potential is to achieve complete identification with the Presence, so you serve as an open door for it to express itself in the material world. Your spiritual identity and individuality is anchored in your I AM Presence, which means it could never be destroyed no matter what happens to you on earth.

IDENTITY BODY

An aspect of your aura/mind that houses your sense of identity.

IMMACULATE CONCEPT OR VISION

This refers to the vision of the highest potential or a pure vision that is not polluted by duality. For example, Mother Mary held the immaculate vision that Jesus would fulfill his mission.

JESUS

The ascended master Jesus was the hierarch or leader for the Age of Pisces. He holds the office of planetary Christ, and we cannot ascend without going through this office. This means that all people need to make peace with Jesus – by transcending the distorted images of Christ created on earth – in order to ascend.

JUDGMENT

There is a group of ascended masters, called the Great Karmic Board, who oversee the overall planetary growth. One of their tasks is to determine which lifestreams are allowed to embody on earth and for how long. When a being falls into duality, it is assigned a certain time to turn around and start the path back to God. However, if a being violates the free will of other beings, this time can be shortened. The being is then judged by its own actions. However, the ascended masters also teach that it is lawful for people in embodiment to call forth the judgment of fallen beings. If such beings will not change, then the Karmic Board can authorize their removal from embodiment.

Take note that the concept of judgment is not the same as the kind of value-laden judgment exercised by beings trapped in the duality consciousness. Such beings judge based on their own state of consciousness, often labeling as evil anything they do not understand or agree with. This is what Jesus called judging after appearances.

INITIATION

A gradual process whereby you raise your consciousness towards the Christ consciousness. This can be an individual process, where you are guided from within, but it usually involves you following an outer teaching or even a guru or organization.

KARMA

Everything is energy, so whatever we do – even what we think and feel – is done by using energy. We receive this energy as a gift from the I AM Presence. The energy we receive is pure, but we will qualify it according to the contents of the four levels of our minds. We are responsible for our use of energy, and misqualified energy becomes stored in both our auras and in the Akashic records as karma. In order for us to ascend, we must balance all energy by raising it to its original vibration.

The masters have also given a deeper understanding of karma, where karma is the images we hold in the four levels of our minds. Because we see everything through the filter of these energies, we are constantly qualifying energy. Yet we have the option to, at any time, examine our mental images and transcend limiting images—which is truly the path to Christhood, where we accept our divine identity.

This gives us two ways to balance karma. We can invoke spiritual energy through decrees and invocations and requalify the energy from our present level of consciousness. This is possible, but it is a slow process because we are constantly making more karma. The faster way is to work on transcending the mental images, so we stop making new karma. Once we achieve this, we can then balance all remaining karma much faster, because our higher state of consciousness allows us to invoke more energy.

LEMURIA

A continent in the Pacific Ocean that had a high civilization but was destroyed about 12,000 years ago. It is often called the Mother land because it is said to have had a very high spiritual focus for the Divine Mother. The decline of Lemuria started when a group of fallen beings murdered the embodied representative of the Divine Mother.

LIFESTREAM

A term used for an individual self-aware being. It is often used instead of "soul," as a lifestream refers to parts of our beings that are beyond the soul, including the I AM Presence and the lineage of spiritual beings leading all the way to the Creator.

LIGHT

Usually refers to spiritual light, meaning energy that vibrates at higher levels than the energy that makes up the material realm.

LIVING CHRIST

A person who has attained some level of Christ consciousness while still in embodiment.

LIVING WORD

Refers to written or spoken word that is inspired from a higher source and endowed with spiritual light. Words can become cups or chalices that carry spiritual light. This is also called fohat.

LUCIFER

A being who rebelled against God in a previous sphere. Thus, it is considered that Lucifer was the first being to fall into the duality consciousness.

MAITREYA

The ascended master who was the leader of the mystery school called the Garden of Eden. He is considered the Great Initiator, because his initiations are not obvious, and we often do not see that we are being tested. Lord Maitreya holds the office of Cosmic Christ.

GOD THE MOTHER

Another word for the Divine Mother, but can also refer to the feminine aspect of God, which is the entire world of form. We are part of God the Mother.

MASS CONSCIOUSNESS

Every human being has an aura, a personal energy field. Yet the entire planet also has an aura, and within it we find a combination of the individual energy fields of all people embodying on earth. There are certain divisions within this collective or mass consciousness, but all people are affected by the greater whole to some degree. There is a stage on the spiritual path, where our main task is to pull ourselves above the magnetic pull of the mass consciousness, so we can express our individuality.

MATTER, MATERIAL UNIVERSE

Everything is made from energy, so the entire world of form is made from energies of various vibrational qualities. One can create a continuum of vibrations, ranging from the highest level, the level of the Creator, to the lowest. In between one can define several divisions, compartments or octaves of vibrations. For example, one major division is between the spiritual realm and the material realm.

There are several divisions in the spiritual realm, whereas in the material realm there are four divisions. They are, from higher to lower vibrations:
  -the etheric or identity level
  -the mental level
  -the emotional level
  -the physical level

MA-TER LIGHT

The cosmic base energy out of which everything that has form is created. It has no form in itself, but has the capacity to take on any form. It also has a certain basic form of consciousness, which among other characteristics has a built-in striving for its source, the Creator.

The Ma-ter light has been stepped down in vibration to create succeeding spheres. We live in the seventh of these spheres, and the six previous ones have all ascended, becoming part of the spiritual realm.

MENTAL BODY

An aspect of your aura/mind that houses your thoughts and mental energies.

MESSENGER

A person who has been trained to receive teachings and dictations from the ascended realm through the agency of the Holy Spirit.

MISQUALIFICATION

Everything we do, feel or think is done with energy We receive this energy from the I AM Presence and then qualify it with a certain vibration. Anything below the vibration of love is a misqualification and creates karma.

MOTHER, HATRED OF

The Ma-ter light forms the feminine polarity to the Creator. It allows us to project any mental image upon it we want, and then it faithfully reflects back to us physical circumstances that reflect the images in our consciousness. When people enter the fallen consciousness, they cannot take responsibility for themselves, meaning they will not recognize that the Mother can only reflect back what we project upon it and is not seeking to punish us. Instead, such beings feel like victims, and they do feel like matter, the Mother element, is seeking to punish them or prevent them from doing what they want. Thus, they can develop hatred of the mother. Yet since we are all part of the mother aspect of God, hatred of the Mother is a form of self-hatred.

MOTHER MARY

The ascended Master who was embodied as the mother of Jesus. She holds the Office of the Divine Mother for earth.

MYSTERY SCHOOL

An environment designed to present self-aware beings with initiations aimed at raising their consciousness. It is usually overseen by an ascended master of high attainment.

ONENESS

Before the Creator had created any form, there was only the Creator. Thus, a Creator cannot create anything that is separated from itself; it must create everything out of its own being. It does this by manifesting its being as the Ma-ter light and thus taking on whatever form is projected upon it by self-aware beings with free will. Thus, beneath any form, any appearance, there is still the oneness of the Creator. Separation from God is always an illusion, and it is this final illusion we must overcome before we can ascend.

PATH

The masters teach that the ultimate goal of life on earth is to manifest the Christ consciousness, which allows us to permanently ascend to the spiritual realm and become ascended masters. Yet we are originally created at a much lower state of consciousness, and thus we follow a gradual path that raises our consciousness to the ultimate level. The masters say there are 144 different levels of consciousness that are possible for people on earth. You can ascend only after reaching the 144th level.

PHYSICAL BODY, PHYSICAL MIND

Obviously, this refers to the body. The physical mind is that part of the brain and nervous system that is designed to regulate the functions of the body, even prompting us to take care of the needs of the body. This is what gives us certain instinctual cravings for protection, food, sex and other physical needs.

There is nothing inherently wrong with taking care of the needs of the body, but the physical mind is not capable up limiting these needs. Thus, if we do not take command over the physical mind, all of our attention and energy can be spent on fulfilling the needs of the body, leaving nothing left over for spiritual growth.

RAYS, OR SPIRITUAL RAYS

Everything is made from energy. Even Einstein's famous equation, $E=mc^2$, says that matter is created from a very high form of energy that is reduced in vibration by a factor (the speed of light squared). The masters teach that while Einstein's theory is basically correct, there are seven of these reduction factors. In other words, the material universe is made from seven types of spiritual energy that are combined to form all phenomena in the material realm. These types of energy are called rays or spiritual rays. There is a total of 15 rays used to build the entire world of form.

RETREATS

Many ascended masters have a spiritual retreat that exists in the etheric or identity realm. We can make a call to go to such retreats in our finer bodies while our physical bodies sleep at night. A retreat is usually located over a physical location on earth, yet because the retreat is in the etheric realm, it cannot be detected through physical means. A retreat focuses certain spiritual energies that are released to earth. It can also be a focus for giving specific teachings to people who are ready.

SANGHA OF THE BUDDHA

The community of people dedicated to walking the path towards Christhood and Buddhahood. Not limited to a single organization.

SATAN

In its most specific meaning, Satan was one of the beings who fell with Lucifer in a previous sphere. However, in a more general meaning, Satan is a state of consciousness that prompts, forces or tempts us to adapt to current conditions in the material realm.

We were created to be co-creators with God and have dominion over the earth. As Jesus said, "with God all things are possible." Satan is a consciousness that wants to prevent us from exercising our highest potential by causing us to voluntarily limit our creative powers and accepting that current conditions cannot or should not be changed.

The role of the Living Christ is to demonstrate to people that we can transcend the consciousness of Satan. That is why Jesus rebuked Peter when Peter wanted Jesus to conform to his expectations. Jesus said: "Get thee behind me, Satan."

SANAT KUMARA

An ascended master of high attainment. In a previous age, so many people on earth had descended so far into the duality consciousness, that the Karmic Board and other cosmic councils had determined that the earth was no longer a viable platform for growth and thus would be allowed to self-destruct. Sanat Kumara then came with 144,000 lifestreams from Venus in order to hold the spiritual balance until enough people on earth had been raised in consciousness, to where they could hold the balance for the planet.

Many of the 144,000 lifestreams that came with Sanat Kumara are still in embodiment and they are often very spiritual people with a great desire to help other people or improve the world. Yet there can come a point, where such people will hold back their own ascensions unless they let go of the desire to help or change others.

SERPENT

A symbol for a certain state of consciousness that induces doubt into our minds. The specific purpose is to create a division in our beings, so we start to distrust our divine direction, our intuition, our own inner knowing and our spiritual teachers. Can also refer to a specific group of fallen beings.

SERPENTINE LIE, PLOT

The primary serpentine lie is that the Christ consciousness either does not exist or is not attainable for us. Instead, the ultimate reality is the duality consciousness, in which we set ourselves up as gods, who believe we have the right and the capacity to define good and evil by ourselves. This inevitably causes a relative definition of good and evil, because good is seen as that which confirms our existing beliefs and desires, whereas anything that challenges them is labeled as evil.

The serpentine plot is to either get us so paralyzed by doubt that we blindly follow the fallen beings, or to get us so blinded by spiritual pride that we really do believe we are always right. In the latter case, we are also following the leadership of the fallen consciousness, which is in complete opposition to the Christ. We now seek to raise the ego to a godlike status, instead of seeking the Christ consciousness as a means to raising all life.

One aspect of the serpentine plot is to get us to believe that even God can be fit into a dualistic world view. God is portrayed as the opposite of evil or the devil. Thus, we are tempted to believe that in order to further God's cause, it is acceptable to do evil, including killing other people. History has many examples of how people have been deceived into fighting these epic battles against a self-defined evil. In order to win this final victory for good, it is necessary and justified to commit this ultimate act of destroying the enemy. In reality, such struggles only serve to misqualify more energy, that feeds the dark forces and thus give them power to deceive people into continuing the endless struggle. The only way out is the Christ consciousness that sees the oneness of all life.

SHIVA

Traditionally a part of the Hindu trinity. However, the deeper meaning is that Shiva is a cosmic being who is especially helpful for cutting us free from dark forces and the astral plane. We can make a very effective call to Shiva by simply repeating his name 9, 33 or 144 times.

SIN

In ascended master terminology the same as karma, meaning misqualified energy that we need to balance before we can ascend.

SPIRITUAL RAYS

Everything is made from energy. Even Einstein's famous equation, $E=mc^2$, says that matter is created from a very high form of energy that is reduced in vibration by a factor (the speed of light squared). The masters teach that while Einstein's theory is basically correct, there are seven of these reduction factors. In other words, the material universe is made from seven types of spiritual energy that are combined to form all phenomena in the material realm. These types of energy are called rays or spiritual rays. There is a total of 15 rays used to build the entire world of form.

SOUL

The ascended masters sometimes use this word as it is commonly used, namely as that part of our beings that reincarnates. However, the masters also give a deeper understanding, namely that it is the Conscious You that originally descended into embodiment. The soul is a vehicle that the Conscious You has created in order to express itself in this world, and it is often highly affected by the duality consciousness.

Jesus' crucifixion is a symbol for the fact that the Conscious You is crucified (paralyzed) by its own creation. Thus, the soul cannot be raised up or perfected. The soul is made from limiting beliefs and misqualified energies. As the energies are requalified and as the Conscious You transcends the limiting beliefs, the soul gradually dies, until the Conscious You gives up the Ghost of the final illusion of separation. The Conscious You can then claim its true identity as an extension of the I AM Presence and can ascend.

SPHERES

The world of form was created by the Creator defining a spherical boundary and withdrawing its being into a singularity in the center of a void. The Creator then created a sphere in the void by using the Ma-ter light. The Creator defined structures in that sphere and projected self-aware extensions of itself into it. As these extensions grew in awareness, they raised the vibration of their sphere until it ascended and formed the first sphere in the spiritual realm. The Creator then created a second sphere, and the ascended masters from the first sphere then defined structures and sent extensions of their own beings into the second sphere.

This process of one sphere ascending and a new sphere being created has continued, so that we now exist in the seventh such sphere. In the first three spheres, all beings ascended without going into the consciousness of separation and duality. Yet in the fourth sphere, some beings refused to ascend, and they became the first fallen beings. As the fourth sphere ascended, these fallen beings could not ascend, and thus they "fell" into the sixth sphere. Because the newly created sphere had a generally lower vibration, the fallen beings could still exist there. This fact is the basic explanation for the existence of evil in our world.

SPOKEN WORD, SACRED WORD

The spoken word is a technique whereby we use the human voice to invoke spiritual light or energy.

SAINT GERMAIN

An ascended master who is the leader for the coming Age of Aquarius. He also represents the seventh spiritual ray, the ray of freedom. Thus, he is sometimes referred to as the "God of Freedom for the earth." Saint Germain will play an important role for the coming 2,000 years and he has a plan for taking the earth into a Golden Age.

THREEFOLD FLAME, SEVENFOLD FLAME

Everything is energy, meaning your physical body and conscious mind can survive only because you are receiving spiritual light from your I AM Presence. This light descends into your aura, into a chakra that is behind the heart chakra and called the secret chamber of the heart. The light is first manifest as a tiny white sphere, but then splits into a "flame" with three plumes, a blue representing will and power, a yellow, representing wisdom and a pink, representing love.

These three flames correspond to the first of the spiritual rays, with the white sphere corresponding to the fourth ray. When you go into duality, you begin to express the basic creative powers in an unbalanced manner, which causes your threefold flame to become unbalanced. This limits your creative powers, and you cannot grow beyond a certain level on the path to Christhood until you have balanced the threefold flame and attained the purity of motive of the fourth ray. At that point, you can begin to work on the initiations of the 5th, 6th and 7th rays, whereby you gradually develop a sevenfold flame.

TRANSFIGURATION

A spiritual initiation on the path to Christhood. It signifies that you transcend identification with the physical body and its limitations.

TWIN FLAME

The Creator is beyond form. Yet as the first act of creation, the Creator expressed itself as two polarities, masculine or expansive and feminine or contracting. These two basic polarities are represented by two cosmic beings, called Alpha and Omega. In the spiritual realm, we find many beings, who form a polarity of masculine and feminine. For example, Elohim and Archangels all have a masculine-feminine polarity.

There is a popular belief that our souls were created in such a polarity, and thus each of us has a twin flame, who would supposedly be the perfect companion and complete us. Unfortunately, this has led to many romantic notions of finding the perfect love. It is necessary to balance this with the fact that you ascend as an individual being, not with your twin flame. Thus, the path of the ascension is a path whereby you become spiritually complete and self-sufficient, being able to ascend completely with your internal power.

UNASCENDED BEING

A being that has not yet qualified for the ascension, and thus cannot abide in the spiritual realm. This does not only refer to human beings in embodiment. There are unascended beings in all four realms of the material world. For example, many souls who have ties to the astral plane can descend there between embodiments or can become permanently stuck there, not being able to reembody. We human beings can make calls for the cutting free of all unascended beings, so they can move on to the next station on their path.

UNCONDITIONALITY, UNCONDITIONAL LOVE

The duality consciousness operates by creating two opposites. Note that the original divine polarity of expanding and contracting are not opposite but complementary forces. Yet when these concepts are colored by the duality consciousness, they will seem like opposites. This is then coupled with a value judgment, labeling one opposite as good and the other as evil. This is what gives rise to all judgmentalness and discrimination found on earth.

When you attain Christ consciousness, you see that all this is an illusion, because the underlying reality is that all life is one and came from the same source. Thus, you see that God's reality is beyond any of the conditions and value judgments defined by the duality consciousness. It is difficult to describe the non-dual reality with words, but the most commonly used word is to say that God's qualities are unconditional, meaning beyond dualistic conditions.

For example, human love is always conditional. People have to do something right and avoid doing something wrong in order to be worthy to receive love. In God's eyes, you are worthy to receive God's love by the mere fact that you were created as an extension of the Creator's Being. Thus, you do not have to do anything to receive God's love, and nothing you do can make you unworthy of it. God's love is unconditional; beyond conditions.

VIOLET FLAME

A spiritual energy that is especially efficient for transmuting karma or misqualified energy. Saint Germain received a cosmic dispensation to reveal the violet flame in the 1930s. Since then, ascended master students have been invoking it through decrees, invocations and affirmations.

However, it is important to realize that the violet flame can be misused. Misqualified energy is caused by a limiting belief. The energy gradually accumulates in your aura, making you feel burdened. You can invoke the violet flame without changing the limiting belief, which will make you feel better in the short run. However, if you do not change the belief, you will continue to misqualify energy. And if you continue to use the violet flame to transmute the energy, you are misusing Saint Germain's dispensation, because you are not attaining long-term spiritual growth.

About the Author

Kim Michaels is a contemporary spiritual teacher and the author of many popular books about mystical Christianity, self-help and the universal path beyond the human ego and the duality consciousness. He writes with uncomplicated clarity about how to apply the timeless wisdom and gnosis from eastern and western spiritual masters to our daily challenges. Kim has founded 4 inspirational spiritual websites:

transcendencetoolbox.com - practical spiritual tools for invoking light and transcending the limitations of the ego consciousness.

askrealjesus.com - original mystical teachings from Jesus.

ascendedmasteranswers.com - Ascended master answers about various topics.

ascendedmasterlight.com - Ascended master teachings and dictations about everything related to spiritual growth.

www.ingramcontent.com/pod-product-compliance
Lightning Source LLC
Chambersburg PA
CBHW070341100426
42812CB00005B/1387